SCÉAL

SCÉAL

Seasonal Recipes and Stories
from a Modern Irish Bakery

Charlotte Leonard-Kane
and Shane Palmer

Photography by Shantanu Starick

Quadrille

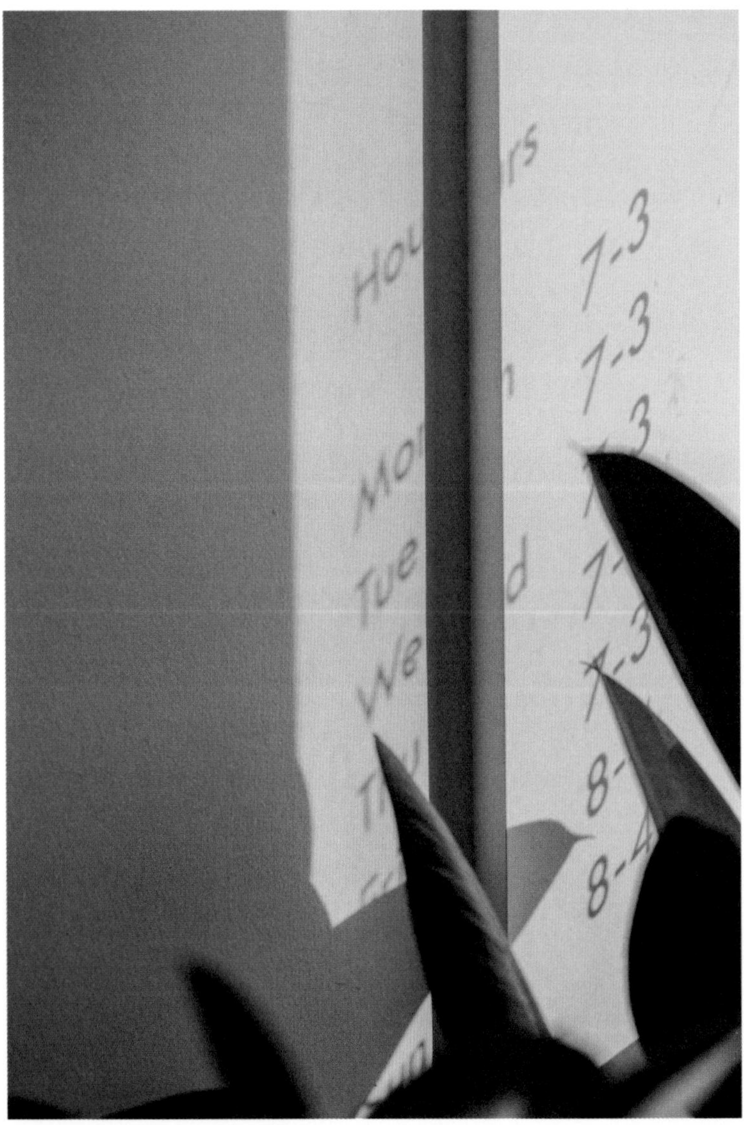

INTRODUCTION

***Scéal*, the Irish for 'story' or 'a tale'**

Scéal is also the name of our artisan bakery, nestled on the east coast of Ireland. I'm Charlotte, and together with my partner, Shane, I've created a charming bakery in the picturesque coastal town of Greystones, County Wicklow. What began as a shared passion for baking has quickly grown into a beacon of baking excellence, a place where we gather inspiration, exchange ideas, share meals and focus on providing our customers with lovingly prepared breads and pastries.

Seasonally driven produce is essential when we are developing new menu items. During summer, we celebrate Irish berries and rhubarb, then we transition to stone fruits and blackberries in autumn, and enjoy apples, quince and pears as we move into the colder winter months. In the depths of winter, we rely on our freezer stock of berries and the brightness of imported citrus to bring some sunshine to our days.

At Scéal Bakery, we have never lost sight of our wonderful customers. Families grew in front of our eyes, bumps to babies. Our core principles have remained unchanged over the years: a devotion to excellence, a focus on community and a passion for crafting culinary narratives that transcend mere sustenance. Where every creation is a chapter in our shared story.

Scéal Bakery is a haven of warmth and inclusivity, reflecting the heart of Irish hospitality. We open our doors to all walks of life, extending an invitation to partake in the joy of craftsmanship and community and the timeless pleasure of breaking bread together.

How it all began

What follows is not the most straightforward story of how to start and run a bakery, but that of two steely and stubborn people who didn't give up on their dream to open a neighbourhood bakery. Let me tell you a tale of two Irish bakers …

A love of food was engrained in both of us from early childhood. Shane grew up in the Irish countryside, in the Queen's County, Laois, in the heartland of Ireland. He was surrounded by vast open spaces, rolling hills, woodlands and fields of cereal crops and vegetables. Coming from a large family, with three generations all sitting around the table for most meals, cooking and baking was essential to keeping hungry mouths fed. Shane's Granny Dunne would bake six loaves of brown bread a day and could effortlessly prepare meals out of a small scullery kitchen for 18 people at a time. Shane spent many afternoons watching his granny cook, peeling carrots and potatoes for the giant family pot of stew and learning her ways around the kitchen. Rarely using weighing scales, Granny just knew her measurements like the palm of her hand. She used her hands as if they were a set of measuring spoons. Most importantly, she used her intuition, relying on her hands and eyes to guide and feel her way through her repertoire.

I, on the other hand, grew up in the city. I learned to cook and bake as a young child sitting on our kitchen draining board, my own small mixing bowl between my legs, eagerly watching Mimi at the cutting board beside me. Every meal was prepared from scratch at home. My siblings and I were lucky enough to grow up with three parents: my mum and dad, and Mimi. Mimi lived with us for nearly two decades, moving in when my brother Ben was a week old to help with childcare and leaving 19 years later when she met the love of her life. How can you put a name or title on someone who is that important to you – a mother, aunt, sister, best friend, mentor and biggest cheerleader all wrapped up into one? The answer is, you can't. You will see Mimi referenced throughout this book. She taught me the fundamentals of cooking and baking and was the one who gave me the nudge to apply for a culinary arts degree when I lost direction after my Leaving Certificate (the final qualification earned at the end of secondary/high school in Ireland).

Shane and I met on the first day of college, where we were studying for a degree in culinary arts. Placed beside one another alphabetically according to our surnames, Leonard-Kane and Palmer, for our opening kitchen class, we became best friends instantly and, over time, this turned to love. Our very first interaction will be deeply rooted in my memory forever – Shane enthusiastically dicing carrots into a *brunoise*, while telling me stories of growing up on his uncle's carrot farm ... only to slice the top off his finger, which meant I had to bandage it up for him.

That was 2010, and we haven't left each other's side since. We both trained as chefs, me working on pastry sections in Dublin and London, while Shane gravitated towards savoury food. A pivotal moment in our approach to cooking happened to us concurrently in two separate kitchens, in two different parts of the UK, while on internships. I was interning on the pastry section at Petersham Nurseries in Richmond, London, while Shane was on the Dorset coast at River Cottage cookery school. Rooted in both kitchens was fresh, seasonal, local produce. The dessert menu at Petersham would change on a weekly basis, sometimes even daily, depending on what came in from the walled garden and specialist suppliers. River Cottage's head gardener, Will, and the season determined what was in their kitchen day to day. Farm-fresh produce went from the soil to the sink, and from there to the pot, being served to guests from gate to plate that evening.

San Francisco

After graduating with a BA (Hons) in Culinary Arts in 2014, an opportunity to work in San Francisco came our way – the modern-day epicentre of sourdough and patisserie. Jaded from working in kitchens and both wanting to change the direction of our professional careers, we emigrated to the US for a year and a half, devoted to training as bakers.

While in San Francisco, we gained invaluable skills and knowledge working with some of the best bakers in the industry. California and the Bay Area have deep roots in the Slow Food movement started by Alice Waters in the 1970s. It's safe to say that Waters has influenced every aspect of American cooking and cultural norms around food with her approach to the sustainability practices behind food production and food waste. Her farm-to-table restaurant Chez Panisse has an ethos of using local and organic produce, which has seeped into restaurants, bakeries and eateries across the Bay (and worldwide).

Every neighbourhood in the city has a weekly farmers' market, with vendors selling the most incredible local produce. On our days off, Shane and I would cycle to our local market in Bernal Heights, which became a new weekly ritual. I started a job with Craftsman and Wolves, a contemporary patisserie and bakery that was seasonally driven. My first day was in June, the height of stone fruit and berry season. Craftsman and Wolves had a weekly farmers' market stall, selling breads and pastries at the celebrated Ferry Plaza Farmers Market. We had a direct link to the farmers, with the delivery van returning full to the brim with fresh fruits, vegetables, edible flowers and cheeses every Saturday. We'd both been exposed to that same level of connection to the seasons in the UK. I wanted to find that in Ireland.

Shane landed a dream job working as a baker with Nathan Yanko of M.H. Bread and Butter, the previous head baker of Tartine who had recently opened a new bakery 30 minutes north of the Golden Gate Bridge in San Anselmo, Marin County. Over the next year, Shane's lonesome nightly pilgrimage led him across the Golden Gate at 2 a.m. M.H. became his temple of bread.

In the late summer of 2016, we landed back home in Ireland, homesick and jobless. The same question bounced from friend to friend: 'What are your plans now that you're home?' Well, open a bakery, of course. It was all we'd dreamed and spoken about for the last 18 months, but to say it out loud to friends and family was daunting. Chatter began about the possibility of renting a small kitchen in a portable cabin on a one-acre organic smallholding nestled between Glasnevin and Ballymun – a suburb of north Dublin, 15 minutes from the city centre. The first time we visited the farm to view the tiny little kitchen, we were blown away. Like everyone who arrives at Elmhurst Cottage Farm for the first time, we were in awe of its open space, calm air and the sheer peacefulness of the land.

We had little to no savings left in our bank accounts after the move back to Ireland. How could we pay for our deposit on the kitchen, buy the equipment needed to start a microbakery and cover all the other costs of getting a business off the ground? A plan was mapped out to apply for a stall at Dublin's largest Christmas market – the Dublin Flea Christmas Market – selling my beloved Christmas puddings, jars of mincemeat and mince pies. All our hopes centred on raising enough funds to cover the first large payments to get our bakery dream started. We cleared a back room at my parents' house to create a makeshift kitchen space for pudding production. With no commercial oven yet, we bartered our time and skills with our friends Luca and Aisling, owners of The Fumbally café, to allow us to steam oven-loads of puddings once the café was closed in the evenings. In return, I hand-laminated pastries for the café to sell in the mornings and Shane worked a couple of shifts in the kitchen.

Elmhurst Cottage Farm

In the depths of winter in January 2017, Scéal moved into a portable cabin kitchen – no bigger than a garden shed – at Elmhurst Cottage Farm. We shared the space with my best friend who was making bespoke wedding cakes, so space was very tight. We shuffled creatively around our secondhand equipment, invested a small, well-spent sum on a Rofco bread oven and began baking. It was very small to begin with, only a handful of loaves in those first few weeks, but the dream was in motion.

Elmhurst helped shape and root what we hoped Scéal would become. We were surrounded by flavours, colours, textures and smells that directly influenced our choices for new pastries and weekly sourdoughs. There was pure excitement come February when the first rhubarb was ready for harvesting or when the chive flowers began to bloom. During the summer months, we were inundated with crops of blackcurrants, redcurrants, raspberries, loganberries and strawberries and the most incredible 'Hinnonmaki Red' blush-pink gooseberries. The possibilities for market-stall items were endless, and we scribbled notes everywhere for potential flavour combinations. We made batches of jams (jellies), preserves and compotes to try to capture the essences of summer. Elderflower soon began to flower and mornings were spent picking flower heads to be steeped in syrup. The heat sweltered in the small portable cabin, putting my hand-laminating skills to the test.

As the seasons began to shift into the cooler months, so did the bounty of the farm. The berry season ended and we moved towards pears, damsons, apples, quince and earthy, woody herbs. The temperature dropped, easing the stress of juggling hand-laminated books of pastry between the refrigerator and freezer. But we faced the worry of coming in to find dough spilling out over bannetons (proving baskets). As the summer months ended, it was apparent we had outgrown our little bakery. The longing for a shop front deepened.

More space, COVID-19 and our hatch

In September 2017, nearly a year to the day after moving back to Ireland, we relocated to a commercial kitchen in a community enterprise centre in Dublin city. It was a stepping stone; a resting place for what we thought would be 12 months, but which actually turned into six years.

With more space and a larger electricity supply came larger pieces of equipment, and the business steadily grew. Our connection to our baking community deepened with weekly market stalls that moved from one side of the city to the other. Our loyal customers followed us, keeping up with our movements through social media and weekly newsletters. A consistent weekend market gave us the chance to build on our menu and the variety of pastries and sourdough we could produce. The Scéal menu expanded, with a serious spiel required to rattle off all the items to each customer in the line for our rotating seasonal items and market specials.

We made tens of thousands of pastries and loaves in that space. It was hard graft packing baked goods into crates and pulling and dragging a market stall setup in and out of the van, all while setting our alarm for 2 a.m. baking shifts. The thing about packing pastries and sourdough loaves into crates and boxes for a market stall, though, is that is they never arrived with our customer in the way that we wanted them to experience them – the crusts on loaves were a little cracked, toppings on Danish pastries were scattered and bruised, cream fillings collapsing. We craved our own bakery space where pastries could be served on plates, loaves displayed on the shelves still warm from the oven and a refined coffee menu could be served to tie it all together. Towards the end of 2019, we started to focus our energy on finding a permanent home for Scéal Bakery.

Everyone knows what happens next. March 2020 – the world shut down with the arrival of the global pandemic. Within a couple of days we lost all our market stalls. Our lifeline for revenue and reaching customers on a weekly basis had vanished. We closed the business for three months, with nowhere to sell our baked goods, no bricks and mortar shop and our commercial kitchen out of bounds. We had to adapt, rebuilding our website into a pre-order click-and-collect service. We rented a hatch space from The Fumbally café in the heart of Dublin 8. Another stepping stone that was intended to last a couple of months – a short-term plan while we waited for society to open up again.

The next two years turned into an incredibly busy time. We were completely and totally overwhelmed by the response of our customers when we opened the hatch. Our webshop would sell out within minutes. Each week we'd reassess, asking ourselves: 'Could we bake more?' and were taken aback when everything would sell out again.

For three years we sold breads and pastries out of the hatch.

Approaching burnout and completely exhausted, we realised that we couldn't do it all on our own and we recruited a real estate agency to search for our permanent bakery home.

Scéal Bakery: our new home

In the depths of December 2021, the week of Christmas, on a cold, wet, dreary day, we ventured out of Dublin to Wicklow to see a new-build listing that had just come to market. We knew instantly that it was the place. A blank canvas lay before us. Three walls of floor-to-ceiling windows flooded the space with light; a vast, empty rectangle that looked directly onto the harbour and the expanse of the Irish Sea, with glimpses of the headland and jutting cliffs. The wind whipped the sea and the metal masts and rigging of the sailing boats rattled while they swayed in the water, and the tide ebbed and flowed as we walked the perimeter, hashing out ideas and potential layouts. We had to make it work. That week, we presented our proposal to the letting agency. Two years of paperwork, bureaucracy and delayed timelines then lay ahead of us.

All the while, life continues and has a funny way of filling your plate with just as much as you can handle before tipping the scales. A baby, a bakery and a book at the same time. I was 33 weeks pregnant when we were handed the keys to our new bakery in Greystones, County Wicklow. Thirty-six weeks when the contractors landed on site to begin the fit-out. The walk-in refrigerator was installed the day I gave birth. Work on site paused for a moment while Shane and I adjusted to life as three with our daughter, Robin Mimi.

Working closely with a design studio, we planned the layout, keeping the space completely open. This was for two reasons: to allow our team of pastry chefs and bakers to see the harbour, the sky and water and to have direct access to natural light. And for our customers to see the hands that made their daily loaves and pastries. Working as a baker can be relentless: unsocial hours, physically tiring and mentally taxing coming to work when the rest of the world is sleeping. In Ireland, open-plan kitchens have become the norm but rarely could you walk into a bakery to see the bakers working, the oven being loaded with bread, folds being performed on croissant dough and pastries being delicately shaped. There is a disconnect in society between where our food comes from and who makes it – we wanted to change that.

With a 12-week-old newborn in arms, we opened the doors of our new home in Greystones. Our team grew from a humble five to 27 dedicated, wonderful and hardworking individuals from all walks of life, all under the same roof to bring our dream of a neighbourhood bakery to reality. Kitchen porters, bakers, pastry chefs, baristas, front-of-house servers and managers. We couldn't have done it without them.

The bakery has become a hub for the local community. Sea swimmers barrelling in to take the big communal table down the back to warm up their hands after a dip in the Baltic-cold Irish Sea. New mums gathering for coffees and collective support in their new lives. Dog walkers, kids scooting and seasoned hikers all traverse our front door on the marina.

All the while, we are busy working away inside, watching the tide come in and out. Bliss.

SPELT &
SUNFLOWER
SEEDS
SESAME
MISO

Equipment

The essentials

Digital scales
A set of digital scales is vital for accurate baking and measuring. Measuring by weight – in grams and kilograms or pounds and ounces rather than cups – is needed throughout this book. Digital scales are one of the most important tools in your baking kit.

Digital thermometer
This is used throughout the book for everything from checking the internal temperatures of baked loaves to cooking out custards and fillings.

Dough/bench scraper
Available online and from good kitchen shops, these scrapers come with plastic or wooden handles. I gravitate towards the wooden-handled ones as they are more tactile. Use for dividing dough, rounding off balls, scooping up ingredients and transferring them to bowls or containers. They help keep your hands clean. An added bonus is that they are great for cleaning down work surfaces and cuttings boards.

Bowl scraper
A flexible, plastic bowl scraper with rounded edges is very handy for cleaning down the edges of mixing bowls, scraping doughs from work surfaces and transferring fillings to piping (pastry) bags.

Rolling pin
A sturdy rolling pin will be part of your kitchen for years, if not decades, to come. I use a straight, dowel-style rolling pin. The tapered-ended, patisserie-style pins are a nice-to-have. I would avoid rolling pins that spin on handles as this makes them hard to control in terms of pressure and accuracy.

Measuring tape
My new favourite piece of kit. A standard fabric measuring tape that is double-sided – inches on one side, centimetres on the reverse. You can find them in most supermarkets or fabric shops. If not, then a 30 cm (12 in) ruler is also very helpful. I use it religiously for measuring croissant shapes and sizes.

Rubber spatulas and wooden spoons
Have at least one of each in your kitchen. If you're feeling generous, I would have a selection of sizes of both.

Whisk
One good metal whisk is all you need. Pick one with heavy, overlapping wires as it will speed up whipping and aerating by hand.

Mixing bowls
I lean towards metal bowls for longevity. Tempered glass bowls are fine, but they can chip. A selection of small, medium and large bowls is helpful for weighing up recipes, measuring, mixing, resting and cooling. For making sourdough at home, I like to use a large ceramic bowl as it maintains its temperature more consistently.

Baking trays (pans)
The standard baking tray used for this book is heavy-based and 40 x 30 cm (16 x 12 in) in size. It fits nicely in the refrigerator and directly on the racks in my home oven. A variety of baking tray sizes is helpful. Our focaccia calls for a smaller tray, measuring 28 x 36 cm (11 x 14 in).

Loaf tins (pans)
I tried to keep all recipes in this book to one size of loaf pan for ease – 23 x 13 cm (9 x 5 in), 900 g (2 lb) with straight edges.

Large and small saucepans
You'll need these more than you think. Many of the recipes have a hob (stovetop) element, whether its making jams (jellies), custards, choux pastry or brown butter.

Pastry brush
You'll want at least one pastry brush with natural bristles in your kitchen kit. Make sure to clean and dry it properly between each use. Particularly after egg washing croissants.

Bakeware and cake tins (pans)
A 24 cm (9½ in) and 20 cm (8 in) diameter fluted tart tin (pan) and 20 cm (8 in) tall cake tin (springform or loose bottom).

Casserole dish (Dutch oven)
A cast-iron casserole dish with a heavy lid is an essential piece of equipment for baking sourdough at home. Don't buy an expensive one, as the enamel chips due to the high heat that you will be baking at. This pot will be dedicated to baking sourdough – it'll tarnish, blacken and wear with use.

Silicone muffin cases
These are used for blind baking the centre of our Danish pastries. They are widely available online and from specialist baking retailers. The ones we use in the bakery are 7 cm (2¾ in) in diameter and 4 cm (1½ in) tall. They are sometimes called mini muffin moulds. We fill the centres with dried chickpeas (garbanzos) to use as as baking beans (pie weights).

Nice-to-haves

Reusable piping (pastry) bags
You'll be surprised how many times you'll reach for a piping bag when baking, whether for piping choux pastry, filling pastries or decorating cakes. Disposable ones are also available, but I try to minimise my use of single-use plastics.

Piping nozzles (tips)
Have a selection of different sizes with round and star-shaped nozzles.

Stand mixer
This is an investment piece, so do some research. We all know the big brand names. I use a stand mixer with a bowl-lift stand rather than a tilt head. I find it easier to scrape down the sides of the bowl this way. You'll need a metal bowl with 6.6-litre (9-quart) capacity and three mixing attachments: whisk, paddle and dough hook.

Bannetons
Amateur bread bakers should have at least one banneton in their kitchen cabinet. It is essential for the long, slow prove of sourdough. They are produced from many different materials now, depending on your budget – wooden pulp, plastic, rattan, woven wicker. Aim for a capacity of 1 kg (2 lb 4 oz). If you don't have a banneton, you can make your own with a clean dish towel and medium mixing bowl. When selecting the banneton shape, make sure it aligns with your casserole dish (Dutch oven) dimensions. If you have a round dish, buy a round banneton; if you have an oval-shaped dish, buy an oval banneton.

Cookie scoop
After training as a baker in the US, a cookie scoop became an important part of my baking kit. Your cookies will be uniform and your hands clean. If you don't have a cookie scoop, you can roll our cookie recipes with the palms of your hands.

Small offset spatula
The pastry chef in me has silly amount of offset spatulas laying around. Just one is needed. I find them essential for so many tasks, from spreading fillings and removing loaves from loaf pans to lifting baked cookies from baking trays (pans).

Baking beans (pie weights)
We use dried chickpeas (garbanzos) in the bakery as our weight for blind baking. They are a fraction of the price of ceramic baking beans and do the same job. Rice, lentils and other dried beans work well too.

A note on weighing ingredients

For all the recipes, we are strong believers in weighing everything in grams, using a set of digital scales. It is the most accurate way to weigh ingredients for baking consistency and success. We also weigh liquids in grams rather than measuring them in millilitres or US cups. We do, however, provide pound and ounce equivalents in decimals and occasionally teaspoon and tablespoon measurements in the recipes.

A note on oven temperatures

All oven temperatures in the book refer to fan ovens.

Raw Buckwheat 06-09
Rosemary Garlic Oil 06-09
Chickpeas 06-09
Polenta 06-09
Lentils 06-09
Walnuts 06-09
Poppy Seeds 06-09

Ingredients

Flour

Flour is the backbone of baking, and understanding its types and protein content is essential for choosing the right flour for your recipe. Protein content determines how much gluten a flour can form, influencing structure, texture and overall results. Protein content in flour represents the percentage of proteins, including glutenin and gliadin, which combine to form gluten when hydrated. Gluten gives elasticity and structure to doughs, making it a crucial factor in baking croissants and sourdough.

Checking the protein content on bags of flour matters (you'll find it in the nutritional information label). It impacts structure – higher-protein flours create strong, elastic doughs that are ideal for sourdough and focaccia. Next is texture – lower-protein flours produce tender baked goods, which you want for biscuits (cookies) and pastry. When mixing and baking doughs, note that high-protein flours absorb more water than low-protein flours, which will affect the consistency of the dough.

Understanding flour and protein content gives you the freedom to experiment. You can blend different flours to create distinct flavour profiles and texture. When switching flours, be mindful that you account for different hydration needs.

Note that you will need plain (all-purpose) flour at home for dusting work surfaces when making breads and pastries.

Sourcing flours
Your local health food shop is a wonderful resource for good-quality flours. They will more than likely source organic, locally grown grains, wholegrain and speciality flours. Compared to larger supermarkets, specialist health food shops order in smaller quantites, meaning the flour on the shelf will be fresher.

Flours often have different names depending on where you live. For example, wholemeal flour in the UK is known as whole-wheat flour in the US. I recipe-tested for this book using the Dove's Farm organic flour range, blending different flours to achieve the protein content and desired texture once baked. For example, I blended plain (all-purpose) flour and strong bread flour for roughly 12 per cent protein for our *Croissant Dough* (see page 25).

Note that soft wheat flours grow especially well in Ireland. Try to source Irish-grown and milled flours for your more tender bakes.

Yeast and osmotolerant yeast

Croissant dough is higher in sugar than other doughs and also lower in moisture. In a dough that has a high concentration of sugar, the yeast and sugar compete for water. To allow croissant dough to prove evenly and effectively, bakers and pastry chefs rely on osmotolerant yeast. This is a specific strain of yeast that can thrive when the sugar stockpiles the water cells. If you are going to the effort of making croissants at home, I strongly suggest you purchase a packet of osmotolerant yeast. It is available online from specialist baking websites.

Butter

All the recipes in this book use unsalted butter. This allows you to control the level of salt in your bakes. A standard salted butter in the supermarket is seasoned with 2 per cent salt, but this can vary from brand to brand, leading to inconsistencies. It's a common percentage you see across fermentation as well, as kimchis, sauerkauts and sourdough usually contain 2 per cent salt, too. All our recipes contain salt. Irish butter is the best in the world – with a deeper golden hue from grass-fed cows and a richer mouthfeel with deep, complex flavour and aromas once baked with. Irish butter can be found in many countries now, appearing in most dairy aisles around the world.

Salt

Two types of salt appear throughout this book. Fine sea salt and flaky sea salt. Fine sea salt is used in recipes, whereas flaky salt is kept for finishing and a little extra seasoning, such as in our *Chocolate Chip and Sea Salt Cookies* (see page 154). Salt is interlinked with butter. As mentioned above, all the recipes in this book use unsalted butter. You have the power when you are in control of the salt. Salt is crucial for fermentation. In sourdough and croissants, the presence of salt slows down the activity of yeast cells, ensuring fermentation doesn't happen too quickly. This is a great symbiosis in baking, since slowing down the fermentation allows for more flavour to develop.

Gelatine

The recipes in this book are made using sheet gelatine, which is also what we use in the bakery. I find this easier and quicker to use than powdered gelatine. Sheet gelatine is now widely available in most large supermarkets. Dr Oetker is the main brand you will come across and is what I used.

I list the number of sheets used in a recipe, not the grams. This point is important. Gelatine is available in different strengths, known as the bloom. These are titanium, bronze, silver, gold and platinum. The different types also influence the clarity with which they set a gel – titanium being the cloudiest and platinum the clearest. However, this is where it can become confusing. A common mistake (which I've made too) is to think that the stronger the bloom, the less gelatine is needed in a recipe. Wrong! One sheet of each type of gelatine has the same gel strength, meaning they will all set the same amount of liquid. As long as your recipe is in sheets, not grams, you can substitute 1:1 between the different types of gelatine from whatever you have available to you.

To bloom sheet gelatine, fill a small bowl with cold water. Place the gelatine sheet(s) into the water, ensuring it is fully submerged. Leave to sit for 5 minutes. The sheet will transform from rigid and brittle to soft and gelatinuous. Using your hands, lift the gelatine out of the water and tightly squeeze out any excess water.

When adding gelatine to a recipe, make sure the liquid is hot so that the soft gelatine melts and dissolves evenly. Whisk the gelatine into the liquid to evenly distribute, removing any lumps.

Cream

Ireland has exceptional dairy. Our cream has a higher fat content than single (light) cream in the UK or US. Cream in Ireland is called 'fresh cream' and has a fat content of 38 per cent, whereas single cream in the UK has 18 per cent fat and double (heavy) cream has a fat content of 48 per cent. I would recommend seeking out whipping cream if in the UK, which is roughly 36 per cent, and heavy cream if in the US, which is roughly 36–38 per cent. Double cream will be too rich for the fillings in this book.

Eggs

I recipe tested this book using large (US extra large) free-range eggs from our local supplier, Syl. They are the same eggs we use in the bakery every day. Source the best-quality eggs that are available to you. Another important consideration is their freshness. The weight of whole eggs (out of the shell) and yolks is used in the majority of the recipes in the book. This allows for accuracy in your bakes. We give the approximate weight of individual eggs alongside.

CROISSANT

Notes on Viennoiserie

Viennoiserie refers to a style of baking that has its origins in Vienna, Austria. It is a category of breakfast pastries we all know – croissants, pains au chocolat and Danish pastries. Delicate layers of dough and butter are laminated, creating thin layers of pastry that transform into crisp flakes in the oven.

We start this chapter with a recipe for making croissants, one of the hardest bakes to master at home. There are an incredible number of variables at play in the home kitchen: the temperature, the humidity, the baker's hand-laminating skills, the efficiency of your home refrigerator, the ingredients selected. In the bakery, we control these areas as best we can. We record dough temperatures, use a humidity-controlled refrigerator prover for dough storage and have the luxury of a sheeter for rolling out each fold with precision and speed. It is well worth the extra work to make croissants at home – nothing compares to the deep golden crust and honey crumb of fresh croissants, or the aroma filling the kitchen as they bake.

Butter

Croissants are a true reflection of the ingredients you use. As I mentioned earlier, at Scéal I am steadfast about baking with Irish butter. In my opinion, it is the best in the world, superior to laminating butter from France, the Netherlands and Germany. We have used unsalted Irish butter from the beginning. I tested all the major supermarket Irish brands for laminating – for flavour, plasticity and baking qualities. The butter we produce in Ireland ranges from 80–84 per cent butterfat, which is ideal for lamination.

When hand-laminating, we place a flat sheet of butter – this is the 'butter block' (often referred to as *beurrage*) – in the centre of the dough to create the pastry layers, alternating between dough/butter/dough/butter.

The ideal butter temperature for laminating is 12–14°C (54–57°F). If you want to get really technical about the temperature, check it with a digital thermometer before you start rolling. Intuition is really important here. The more croissants you roll, the more you will understand butter texture and it will become second nature. You are looking for plasticity and flexibility in the butter. You should be able to bend the butter without it melting in your hands (too warm) or snapping (too cold).

If the butter is too cold when you begin laminating, it will break and shatter as you roll it, creating very uneven, indistinguishable layers, and these shards of butter will pierce through the delicate layers.

If the butter is too warm, it will smear and melt into the dough as you try to build your lamination. It is also very likely that if you start laminating with butter that is too warm, it will leak out when baking. Again, this leads to uneven, undefined layers. Your croissant will be bready once baked, almost brioche-like in texture.

Also bear in mind that the minimum resting time between folds is 45 minutes. This is to rest the gluten in the dough but also to chill the butter back down again.

Tips for storing master croissant dough

× After three single folds have been performed, let the dough rest for a minimum of 3 hours and a maximum of 8. After 8 hours, you will begin to see tiny little bubbles – this low-level activity will begin to disrupt the beautiful layers of dough and butter you have created.
× Keep in mind that you will be opening and closing the refrigerator door multiple times on the day you are laminating the croissant dough. Every time the door opens, the temperature will rise.
× Once the dough has been laminated and three single folds completed, you can store the croissant dough in the freezer. Do not store for longer than a week. This is because the longer it is kept in the freezer, the more inactive the yeast cells will become.

Master Recipe:
Croissant Dough

Makes 6–8 pastries, depending on the shape and fillings used
Time 2 days

155 g	(5.5 oz) water
95 g	(3.3 oz) whole milk
10 g	(0.4 oz) osmotolerant yeast
75 g	(2.7 oz) caster (superfine) sugar
12 g	(0.4 oz) fine sea salt
275 g	(9.7 oz) plain (all-purpose) flour, plus extra for dusting
260 g	(9.2 oz) strong white bread flour
32 g	(1.1 oz) unsalted butter (at room temperature)

Butter block

250 g	(8.8 oz) unsalted butter

This recipe is adapted from the one we use at Scéal every day. I have simplified it for home bakers to include plain and strong bread flour as the base of the recipe. There is nothing quite like the aromas of caramelised, brown butter filling the kitchen, and pulling a warm croissant from the oven to enjoy with your morning coffee. Something we've learned over the years is that croissant pastry is a versatile vehicle for adding different fillings, flavours and shapes, which you will see as this chapter progresses.

Before you get started, here is a rough guideline for planning out the three days needed to make croissants at home.

Day one (afternoon):
In the afternoon, mix the croissant dough. You don't want the dough to bulk ferment for longer than 18 hours, so let's do some maths. If you plan on laminating your croissant dough at 8 a.m. on day two, then you will need to mix your dough at 4 p.m. on day one. If you mix the dough at 5 p.m., you have until 9 a.m. to laminate it and so forth.

Day two (morning):
In the morning, remove the dough from the refrigerator and perform three single folds. The dough should rest for a minimum of 45 minutes between each fold, so set aside 3 hours for this step. The dough then has to rest for a further 3 hours before you can move on to shaping your desired pastries.

Day two (afternoon):
Take the laminated book of dough from the refrigerator and roll it out to the required dimensions (given with the recipes). Shape each pastry and return them to the refrigerator to chill overnight.

Day three (morning):
Decide what time you would like to enjoy your pastries, as they will need to prove first. If they are for breakfast at 8 a.m., then set an alarm to get up at 5.30 a.m. Remove the pastries from the refrigerator, brush lightly with egg wash and place in the oven (turned off) for the allotted prove time. This varies from pastry to pastry.

RECIPE CONTINUED OVERLEAF

Day one (morning)

Prepare the butter block

1 Remove the butter for the butter block from the refrigerator and leave to sit for a few hours until it is soft enough for pressing, smoothing and flattening out. You can also leave the butter out to soften the night before making the butter block.

Day one (afternoon)

1 Cut two pieces of baking parchment, each measuring 20 x 20 cm (8 x 8 in). Using a pencil and ruler, mark out a 19 x 19 cm (7½ x 7½ in) square as a guide for the butter block dimensions. Cut the butter block into four equal pieces lengthways.
2 Arrange the butter block pieces tightly beside each other on one of the pieces of baking parchment. Lay the second piece of parchment on top. With a rolling pin and even pressure, push down on the butter until it fills the dimensions of the square. You can tap with the rolling pin to push the butter together. You are aiming to smooth out the gaps between the cut pieces of butter to create one uniform block.
3 Use a bowl scraper to smooth the edges and over the seams. Flip the butter over to check both sides are smooth and uniform.
4 Now fold the edges of the baking parchment tight to the butter block, using the structure of the paper to create flat, level lines on each edge.
5 Push the butter to the edges and smooth the surface with a few rolls back and forth with the rolling pin. Place on a tray and pop into the refrigerator, ideally overnight. You will use this butter block on day two for laminating.

DAY ONE (STEPS 1–3)

PREPARING THE BUTTER BLOCK

Mix the croissant dough

1 Weigh the water and milk into the bowl of a stand mixer. Add the yeast, sugar, salt, both flours and the butter.
2 Using the dough hook attachment, mix on speed 2 for 5 minutes. Increase to speed 5 and mix for 7–9 minutes. The length of the second mix will vary, depending on the gluten development.
3 To check the dough development, after 7 minutes at speed 5, pinch off a small piece of dough and gently stretch it into a square/rectangle between your fingers. Keep stretching the dough until it forms a thin film without tearing. You should be able to see through the dough – if not, mix the dough for another minute at speed 5, then check again.
4 Remove the dough from the bowl and knead gently and very briefly on a clean work surface – only a couple of passes through your hands, so that it comes together. Flatten the dough into a square with the palms of your hands or a rolling pin – it should measure 19–20 cm (7½–8 in) square. Wrap tightly in cling film (plastic wrap) and leave to rest for 10 minutes.
5 Place the dough on a tray and transfer to the refrigerator to slowly ferment. As the dough ferments overnight, it will expand, become puffy and push against the tightly wrapped cling film. This is a great indication that the yeast is active, alive and doing its job. If you notice zero activity in your dough the following morning, start again. At this stage, you have invested a very limited amount of time and ingredients. Starting again now means you will be less likely to be disappointed down the line. Do not exceed 18 hours of bulk fermentation in the refrigerator.

DAY ONE (STEP 4)

PREPARING THE BUTTER BLOCK

Day two (morning)

Laminate the dough

1 Take the butter block from the refrigerator about 15 minutes before you plan to start rolling out the layers of dough. Remember, you want the butter to be flexible and have a bendy plasticity. You can check the temperature of the butter with a digital thermometer – the ideal temperature for laminating is 12–14°C (54–57°F). See page 22 for further advice on butter texture.

2 Remove the dough from the refrigerator and peel off the cling film. Lightly flour the work surface. Pat the dough into a rectangle, removing any large pockets of air from the bulk fermentation. Lightly roll the dough into a rectangle 33 cm (13 in) long and 21 cm (8¼ in) wide.

3 Place the butter block in the centre of the dough. Bring the top and bottom sections of dough over the butter block to meet in the centre. Pinch the seam closed, using your fingers or the palm of your hand. The seam will be facing towards you at this stage, perpendicular to your body.

4 Press the rolling pin along the width of the dough, creating shallow indents. Don't push all the way down. This helps lock the butter and dough together.

5 Now you are going to switch to rolling the dough lengthways. Working confidently and quickly, roll the dough lengthways away from you. Flour very lightly, if necessary. The rectangle should be approximately 55 cm (22 in) long and 5 mm (¼ in) thick. The thickness of the dough is the important measurement here. The length of the rectangle may vary.

6 Using a pizza cutter or sharp knife, cut the short edges of the dough to straighten them and expose the butter. Now you will perform a single fold. Take one third of the dough and fold it up to the centre. Next, take the other third of the dough and fold it over the top.

DAY TWO (STEP 3)

ADDING THE BUTTER BLOCK

7 Using a sharp knife, carefully score the edges where the dough is folded. This helps release tension and will make the next fold easier to roll. Rough dimensions at this stage: 18 x 19 cm (7 x 7½ in) and 3 cm (1¼ in) thick.

8 Wrap the dough in cling film, place on a tray and return to the refrigerator to chill and rest for a minimum of 45 minutes.

9 Remove the dough from the refrigerator and place on the work surface with the open edge facing you. Using as little flour as possible, roll the dough into a rectangle, approximately 50 cm (20 in) long and 5 mm (¼ in) thick. Again, thickness is the important factor here. Cut the short edges to tidy them up and expose the butter layers.

10 Now you will perform a second single fold. Take one third of the dough and fold it up to the centre. Now take the other third and fold it over the top. Using a sharp knife, score the edges where the dough is folded to release the tension. Wrap the dough tightly in cling film, place on a tray and return to the refrigerator to chill and rest for a minimum of 45 minutes. You're nearly there. One more turn to go.

11 Repeat step 9.

12 Now perform a third single fold, the final one. Repeat step 10, this time allowing the dough to rest in the refrigerator for a minimum of 3 hours before shaping. The 3-hour minimum is very important, as it allows the gluten in the dough to relax and the butter to firm up. If you don't rest the dough for this period of time, you will struggle with rolling out in the next stage.

13 Please make sure you have performed three single folds. I'm stressing this here one final time as miscounting the folds can happen to the best of us.

Day two (afternoon)

1 Follow your chosen recipe (pages 31–54) to learn how to cut, shape and prepare your croissants or other pastries before baking and enjoying. Or you can store the croissant dough in the freezer for up to a week, ready to make your pastries another day. (To defrost the dough, take it directly from the freezer to the refrigerator. Do not leave it out on the kitchen counter as it will slowly begin to soften, creating air bubbles in the delicate layers. Defrosting can take anywhere from 12–18 hours, so bear this in mind when planning when to proof and bake the croissants.)

DAY TWO (STEPS 5–6)

PERFORMING A SINGLE FOLD

Irish Butter Croissants

Makes 7 croissants
Time Master recipe + 1 day

Batch of *Croissant Dough* (see page 25)
Egg Wash (see page 209)

There is no hiding behind a croissant. They are a true reflection of your mixing, laminating and proving skills. Take your time with this and enjoy the process. My best advice for shaping a croissant is to watch videos online – there are thousands to choose from.

Day one

1. Laminate the dough, following the instructions on pages 25–29. Ensure you perform three single folds and that the dough has chilled in the refrigerator for a minimum of 3 hours. I'm going to be beating the same drum here, but it's for a reason.
2. While the dough is resting, line a baking tray (pan) or trays with baking parchment.
3. Take the croissant dough from the refrigerator and place it on a very lightly floured work surface. With the folded, open edge parallel with your tummy, roll the dough out in long, even strokes. Move the dough as you are rolling to ensure it doesn't stick to the work surface. If the dough is springing back and you're having a hard time rolling it out, return it to the refrigerator or freezer to rest and relax – 10–15 minutes should be enough. Roll the dough out until it is 28 cm (11 in) wide.
4. Rotate the dough 90 degrees, so the folded, open edge is now either to your left or right when you look down at it. Roll out a 25.5 cm (10 in) wide and 4 mm (¼ in) thick rectangle, about 38 cm (15 in) in length, but the length of the rectangle will vary each time. The thickness and width are the most important dimensions here. Trim the top and bottom of the dough to reveal the lamination and even out the shape.
5. Make and cut seven triangles – the number of pastries will vary depending on the precision of your lamination process, the accuracy of your rolling, the size of the rectangle of dough before trimming down to size and how much you trimmed the dough between each turn. The triangles should be 8.25 cm (3¼ in) on the base and 25 cm (10 in) in length.
6. Now comes the shaping. This can take thousands of pastries to master, so don't be hard on yourself if they don't come out perfectly. Practice and repetition are key for making croissants. Holding the base of the triangle in your dominant hand, stretch the dough between the thumb and index finger of the same hand. If your dough doesn't want to stretch, stop what you're doing, put the pastries back on a baking tray and return to the refrigerator to rest.
7. Once stretched, the croissant will be a long triangle, measuring about 33 cm (13 in). Working from the wide base of the triangle, roll up the dough. Roll tightly to begin with, creating tension. Roll the dough over itself three times and tuck the point of the triangle underneath itself. Place on the lined baking tray and repeat for the other croissants. Cover the tray with cling film (plastic wrap) and return to the refrigerator overnight.

Day two (morning)

1 Croissants can take 2–3 hours to prove. Working backwards, set your alarm. If you would like warm, fresh pastries at 10 a.m., set your alarm for 7 a.m. Prepare the egg wash, take the pastries out of the refrigerator and brush with the egg wash. Leftover egg wash can be stored in an airtight container in the refrigerator for up to five days. Place in the oven but do not turn it on. Leave the croissants to prove for 2–2½ hours. They should be wobbly, inflated and delicate.
2 Remove the proved croissants from the oven. Preheat the oven to 210°C (450°F) and lightly egg wash the croissants again.
3 Put the baking tray(s) in the oven and reduce the temperature to 200°C (425°F). Bake the croissants for 5 minutes, then turn the oven down to 180°C (390°F) and bake for a further 10–11 minutes. If your oven has hot spots, rotate the tray(s) halfway through.
4 Enjoy the croissants warm with salted butter and *Raspberry Jam* (see page 194) or shop-bought jam (jelly).

Twice-baked Almond Croissants

Makes 6 croissants
Time 1–4 days

6 day-old croissants
Brandy Syrup (see page 208)
Flaked (slivered) almonds
Icing (confectioners') sugar, for dusting

For the Crème Pâtissière

125 g	(4.4 oz) whole milk
½	vanilla pod (bean), seeds and pod
60 g	(2 oz) egg (about 1 UK large/US extra-large egg)
12 g	(0.4 oz) cornflour (cornstarch)
30 g	(1 oz) caster (superfine) sugar
1 g	(¼ teaspoon) fine sea salt
15 g	(0.5 oz) softened unsalted butter

For the Toasted Almond Frangipane

55 g	(1.94 oz) flaked (slivered) almonds
90 g	(3.2 oz) icing (confectioners') sugar
90 g	(3.2 oz) softened unsalted butter
50 g	(1.8 oz) whole egg (1 UK large/US extra-large egg)
25 g	egg yolk (about 1 yolk)
15 g	(0.5 oz) plain (all-purpose) flour
55 g	(1.94 oz) ground almonds (almond meal)
1 g	(¼ teaspoon) fine sea salt

These pastries started out as a weekly market stall item in an effort to keep our food waste to a minimum. Croissants take three days to make from start to finish, so we didn't want any unbought ones being thrown away. And so the twice-baked almond croissant was born, quickly becoming our most popular item on the menu, often seeing us making and baking croissants solely for this recipe.

You can, of course, make the initial croissants yourself following our *Irish Butter Croissants* recipe (see page 31), but if you feel like cheating, use day-old croissants from your local bakery or supermarket. Traditionally, these almond croissants are soaked in a rum syrup, but we use brandy instead – it pairs well with the toasted almond frangipane.

Vanilla crème pâtissière (pastry cream) is folded through the almond frangipane at the end, leading to a soft-set bake. This recipe makes more crème pâtissière than you will need, but the excess can be frozen and enjoyed with other desserts.

1. First, make the crème pâtissière by heating the milk and vanilla pod in a saucepan over a low heat. Don't allow the milk to boil – as soon as it just begins to steam, remove the pan from the heat.
2. While the milk is heating, whisk together the egg, cornflour, sugar and salt in a small mixing bowl. Pour one third of the vanilla-infused milk into the egg mixture and briskly whisk together. Pour the mixture back into the saucepan with the remaining milk.
3. Return the pan to a low heat. Whisk the milk and egg mixture for 3–4 minutes until thick and smooth. The mixture should come to a gentle boil with bubbles and blips on the surface. Remove from the heat and whisk in the softened butter.
4. Pour the crème pâtissière into an airtight container and place a piece of baking parchment on the surface to prevent a skin forming on the cream. Allow to cool at room temperature before storing in the refrigerator. The crème pâtissière can be kept refrigerated for a week.
5. Next, make the almond frangipane by toasting the almonds in a frying pan or on a baking tray (pan) in an oven preheated to 160°C (350°F) for 8–10 minutes. Leave to cool.
6. Using a wooden spoon and large mixing bowl, or a stand mixer fitted with the paddle attachment, cream together the icing sugar and softened butter. The mixture should look pale, fluffy and light – this could take 4–5 minutes. Add the whole egg and egg yolk. Beat for 2 minutes on a medium to high speed. Scrape down the sides of the bowl to catch any lumps of butter. Cream for a further 2 minutes. It is common for the mixture to split, so don't be alarmed.
7. Turn the mixer to low and add the flour, ground almonds, salt and toasted almonds. Fold through 130 g (4.6 oz) of the chilled crème pâtissière.
8. Preheat the oven to 160°C (350°F) and line a baking sheet with baking parchment.

9 Cut the day-old croissants in half, keeping the tops with the bottoms because you will be reassembling them before baking.
10 Brush the bottoms of the croissants liberally with the brandy syrup. Using a small cookie scoop or tablespoon, scoop about 50 g (1.8 oz) of the frangipane into the centre of each base. Spread the frangipane evenly into the corners – I find an offset spatula very handy for this.
11 Put the tops back on the croissants, then, using a reusable piping (pastry) bag (or the offset spatula if you don't have one of these), pipe a line of frangipane along the crown of the croissants.
12 Gather the flaked almonds and press in clusters into the frangipane.
13 Bake the croissants for 30 minutes, or until golden and crisp and the frangipane is set and baked through.
14 Remove from the oven and leave the croissants to cool on the baking sheet before dusting with icing sugar.

Pains au Chocolat

Makes 8 pains au chocolat
Time 2 days with Master recipe

Batch of *Croissant Dough* (see page 25)
Egg Wash (see page 209)

16 chocolate batons or 160 g (5.6 oz) dark chocolate (at least 60–70% cocoa solids)

Every week for the last eight years I save myself a Scéal pain au chocolat to enjoy for breakfast on my day off. When I was on maternity leave, I ate a pain au chocolat daily. We use exceptional chocolate from NearyNógs – a bean-to-bar chocolate producer on the Mourne Peninsula in County Down. A 70% dark chocolate with notes of raspberry and cacao nibs, which stands up to the brown-butter, nutty flavours of our croissant dough.

1. Laminate the *dough*, following the instructions on pages 25–29.
2. While the dough is resting, line two baking trays (pans) with baking parchment and set aside. If you're not using chocolate batons, break the dark chocolate into smaller pieces.
3. Take the croissant dough from the refrigerator and place it on a very lightly floured work surface. With the folded, open edge either to your left or right, roll the dough out in long, even strokes. Move the dough as you are rolling to ensure it doesn't stick to the work surface. If the dough is springing back and you're having a hard time rolling it out, return it to the refrigerator or freezer to rest and relax.
4. Rotate the dough 90 degrees, so the folded, open edge is now parallel with your tummy. Roll a rectangle until the dough is 22 cm (8½ in) wide and 5.5 cm (2 in) thick. The length of the rectangle will vary each time. The thickness and width are the most important dimensions here. Trim the top and bottom of the dough to reveal the lamination and even out the shape – the rectangle of dough should now be 20 cm (8 in) wide.
5. Cut out eight smaller rectangles, so each one is 7 cm (2¾ in) wide and 20 cm (8 in) long and 100–110 g (3.5–3.9 oz) in weight.
6. Place two chocolate batons parallel to each other in the top two thirds of each pastry. If you are using chopped dark chocolate, place a tidy pile in the top two thirds instead.
7. Roll the dough into a Swiss-roll (jelly-roll) shape, tucking the chocolate neatly and tightly into the centre.
8. Place four pastries on each baking tray and lightly brush with egg wash. Place the trays in the oven, but do not turn it on. Leave to prove until inflated, soft and delicate. This can take 2–3 hours. Once proved, remove from the oven.
9. Preheat the oven to 200°C (425°F). Lightly egg wash each pastry again. Place the trays in the oven and reduce the temperature to 190°C (400°F). Bake the pains au chocolat for 5 minutes, then turn the oven down to 180°C (390°F) and bake for a further 13 minutes. If your oven has hot spots, rotate the trays halfway through.
10. Enjoy the pains au chocolat slightly cooled from the oven, with the chocolate still melted in the centre. Dip into a milky coffee and gently pull apart the layers.

Rhubarb and Sweet Woodruff Danish

Makes 6–8 Danish pastries
Time Master recipe + 1 day

Batch of *Croissant Dough* (see page 25)
Egg Wash (see page 209)
Rhubarb Compote (see page 191) or good-quality shop-bought rhubarb jam (jelly)
Icing (confectioners') sugar, for dusting

For the Sweet Woodruff Crème Pâtissière

250 g (8.8 oz) whole milk
10 g (0.4 oz) dried sweet woodruff
80 g (2.8 oz) egg yolk (4 UK medium/US large eggs)
50 g (1.8 oz) caster (superfine) sugar
20 g (0.7 oz) cornflour (cornstarch)
Pinch of fine sea salt
25 g (0.9 oz) softened unsalted butter

For the Oven-poached Rhubarb

400 g (14.1 oz) new-season rhubarb
100 g (3.5 oz) water
200 g (7 oz) caster (superfine) sugar
Juice of 1 lemon

For the Ginger Crumble

50 g (1.8 oz) Demerara sugar
50 g (1.8 oz) cold unsalted butter
50 g (1.8 oz) plain (all-purpose) flour
50 g (1.8 oz) ground almonds (almond meal)
5 g (1 teaspoon) ground ginger
Pinch of flaky sea salt

In the bakery we receive the most amazing vibrant-pink rhubarb from Ryan's Rhubarb in County Dublin. I like to grade our rhubarb for different projects: jamming, making compote, poaching, roasting and even dehydrating. Creating this Danish pastry allows us to use the whole stalk without any of the precious pink part going to waste.

Sweet woodruff (*Galium odoratum*) grows wild in woodlands across north Wicklow where our bakery is located. I spotted it at a specialist plant sale several years ago and now grow it successfully in our vegetable patch. When dried, it is reminiscent of fresh hay, toasted almonds and vanilla. Not everyone will be able to find sweet woodruff, but you can replace it with a vanilla pod (bean).

Day one

1. Laminate the dough, following the instructions on pages 25–29. Ensure you perform three single folds and that the dough has chilled in the refrigerator for a minimum of 3 hours.
2. To make the sweet woodruff crème pâtissière, warm the milk and dried woodruff in a saucepan over a medium heat. Bring the milk to just below steaming – the surface will start to steam and shimmer. Remove from the heat and leave to steep for 30 minutes.
3. Return the milk to the heat. While it is steeping, combine the egg yolks, sugar, cornflour and salt in a bowl. Whisk together until lighter in colour and slightly thickened – this will take 1 minute.
4. Pour the milk and woodruff infusion in a smooth, slow stream into the egg mixture. Whisk until combined. Place a fine sieve (strainer) over the same saucepan and strain off the woodruff. Return to a medium heat and whisk continuously until the mixture is thick and bubbly and the cornflour has cooked out – about 2–3 minutes.
5. Remove from the heat and whisk in the butter. Pass through the sieve again and store in an airtight container. The crème pâtissière will keep in the refrigerator for a week.
6. Next, prepare the oven-poached rhubarb. Wash the rhubarb and cut it into 5 cm (2 in) sticks. Try to pick stalks that have the same thickness, so they take the same amount of time to poach.
7. Preheat the oven to 160°C (350°F).
8. Combine the water, sugar and lemon juice in a roasting tin (or ovenproof dish). Add the rhubarb in an even layer, making sure the tin isn't overcrowded. If the rhubarb isn't submerged by the water, add a splash more. Cover the tin tightly with kitchen foil.
9. Poach the rhubarb in the oven for 10 minutes. Check if the pieces are poached by giving them a gentle squeeze or piercing with a knife. If they're still firm, cook for a further 2 minutes until soft. Remove from the oven and leave to cool, then decant into an airtight container. Steep overnight in the refrigerator to intensify the colour. The poached rhubarb can be stored for up to a week.

Day two

1. Follow steps 3 and 4 on page 31 for instructions on rolling out the dough. The rectangle of dough should be 20 cm (8 in) wide and 8 mm (½ in) thick after rolling, then 18 cm (7 in) wide after trimming down.
2. Cut out six to eight pastries, so each one measures 9 x 9 cm (3½ x 3½ in).
3. Place three or four pastries on each baking tray and lightly brush with egg wash. Place the trays in the oven, but do not turn it on. Leave to prove until inflated, soft and delicate. This can take 1½–2 hours. Once proved, remove from the oven.
4. Preheat the oven to 180°C (390°F) and line a baking try with baking parchment.
5. To make the ginger crumble, put all the ingredients into a medium bowl. Rub the butter into the dry ingredients until you have a sandy, crumb-like texture. Switch from rubbing to mixing and pressing the dough together. Scatter onto the prepared tray. Bake for 15 minutes until golden and crisp. Allow to cool before storing in an airtight container.
6. Line two baking trays with baking parchment and set aside. Make weighted parcels with silicone muffin cases and baking beans (pie weights), then set aside.
7. Preheat the oven to 200°C (425°F). While the oven is preheating, press a muffin case filled with baking beans into the centre of each dough square. Lightly egg wash around the edges of each pastry. Place the trays in the oven and bake the pastries for 5 minutes, then turn the oven down to 180°C (390°F) and bake for a further 11 minutes. Rotate the trays halfway through.
8. Remove the pastries from the oven and leave to cool for a few minutes before removing the muffin cases.

To assemble the Danish pastries

1. Spoon a generous tablespoon (25–30 g/0.9 oz) of rhubarb compote into the bottom of the pastry cavities.
2. Transfer the woodruff crème pâtissière to a piping (pastry) bag. Cut a small opening in the tip of the bag and pipe 30–40 g (1–1.4 oz) of crème pâtissière on top of the compote.
3. Gently place two to three pieces of poached rhubarb on top.
4. Finally, nestle some ginger crumble on top of the rhubarb, dust with icing sugar and enjoy.

Scéal Danish

We use our seasonal Danish pastries to highlight and showcase some of the best fruits available in Ireland. This is also an opportunity for us to have a creative outlet as bakers. Viennoiserie production is repetitive and sometimes monotonous and tiresome. Muscle memory kicks in when you're in front of the sheeter, rolling out book after book of pastries and cutting thousands of croissants and pains au chocolat. Seasonal Danish pastries are exciting for us – our brains bubble and tick with ideas for different shapes and garnishes, flavour pairings and new ingredient combinations.

As a rule of thumb, our Danish pastries are built in layers of texture and flavour, so every mouthful is delicious – from the first to the last bite. The bottom layer is usually a tart and acidic jam or compote, then we add a creamy, custardy filling to carry an infusion. Sometimes we lean on tangy strained yoghurt or rich, velvety mascarpone cream for a creamy layer. Finally, we top the pastries with fruit that might be fresh, poached, roasted or glazed. A delicate scattering of crumble brings additional texture, from shards of shortbread cookie to discs of genoise sponge. I'm a firm believer that each fruit should be celebrated in its own way, only using one type so it can sing.

The summer is high season for berries, which we source from family-run fruit farm, Malone. The season kicks off with strawberries and, in quick succession, we have raspberries, gooseberries, loganberries, blackcurrants, redcurrants, blackberries and blueberries.

In the thrill of a new year, blood oranges and citrus arrive, followed soon after by the tart, pink explosion that is forced rhubarb. These are a welcome shift from the indulgence of the festive period and lovingly grown by Ryan's Rhubarb in Oldtown, County Dublin – the sole commercial growers of forced rhubarb in Ireland.

In the spring we tend to rely on last summer's bounty from the freezer, with gooseberries being an excellent, robust berry to defrost for jams or roasting. To bridge the gap between late spring and summer, we'll source Italian and Spanish stone fruits of exceptional quality: think sun-kissed apricots, nectarines and peaches.

The autumn months draw in with the Irish apple harvest, imported Turkish quince and a short pear season. There are also plums, damsons and some of the last stone fruits.

A seasonal Danish pastry could appear on our menu for a couple of weeks when a particular fruit is at its best and then may not reappear for another year. It's always exciting. Here is snippet of a handful of flavours we've paired over the years.

Spring

× Roast strawberries and chamomile
× Apricots and noyaux
× Gooseberry and elderflower

Summer

× Raspberry and fig leaf (see page 46)
× Blackcurrant and blackcurrant leaf
× Blueberry and earl grey tea
× Blackberries and lemon verbena
× Strawberry and fennel pollen

Autumn

× Apple and buckwheat crumble
× Poached pear, saffron and star anise
× Apple, blackberry and bay leaf
× Poached quince and coconut

Winter

× Rhubarb and sweet woodruff (see page 42)
× Rhubarb and rose geranium
× Blood orange and olive oil
× Blood orange and cardamom

Raspberry and Fig Leaf Danish

Makes 6–8 Danish pastries
Time Master recipe + 1 day

Infused Oil (see page 189) made with fig leaves
Batch of *Croissant Dough* (see page 25)
Egg Wash (see page 209)
200 g (7 oz) *Raspberry Jam* (see page 194) or shop-bought raspberry jam (jelly)
300 g (10.6 oz) raspberries

For the Fig Leaf-Infused Whipped Ganache

3 fig leaves or 50 g (1.8 oz) pulp from making the *Infused Oil*
350 g (12.4 oz) cream, plus extra to top up
100 g (3.5 oz) white chocolate
2 sheets of gelatine
Fine sea salt

Variations of this flavour combination have appeared on our menu for several years now. If you rub a fig leaf between your fingers, you'll experience an amazing aroma of coconut, vanilla pods (beans) and sweet, ripe figs. There's something about that slight hint of coconut from the fig leaves combined with tart, floral raspberries that reminds me of a nostalgic mouthful of Jacob's Mikado biscuit (cookie).

Day one

1 There are a few components to make in advance for these Danish pastries to come together at the end. First, make the fig leaf oil and prepare the dough.
2 Now begin steeping the fig leaf infusion for the ganache. If you are using fresh fig leaves, toast them in a dry pan for one minute on each side. The leaves will shrivel and crisp up while toasting, which helps release the natural oils. Put the toasted leaves (or the fig pulp, if using) into a saucepan with the cream over a medium heat and bring to just below boiling point. Remove from the heat and leave to steep for 12–24 hours in the refrigerator.

Day two

1 Line two baking trays (pans) with baking parchment and set aside.
2 Follow steps 3 and 4 on page 31 for instructions on rolling out the croissant dough. The rectangle of dough should be 20 cm (8 in) wide and 8 mm (½ in) thick after rolling, then 18 cm (7 in) wide after trimming down.
3 Cut out six to eight squares, so each one measures 9 x 9 cm (3½ x 3½ in).
4 Place three or four pastries on each baking tray and lightly brush with the egg wash. Put the trays in the oven, but do not turn it on. Leave to prove until inflated, soft and delicate. This can take 1½–2 hours. Once the pastries have proved, remove from the oven.
5 To make the ganache, strain the fig leaves and squeeze out all the cream. Weigh the cream again and, if necessary, top up with fresh cream to a total of 350 g (12.4 oz). The leaves will have absorbed some of the cream during the infusion stage.
6 Bring the cream back to just below boiling point. At the same time, melt the white chocolate over a bain-marie and bloom the gelatine in some cold water.
7 Once the cream is at the right temperature, squeeze the excess water from the gelatine before whisking it into the cream.
8 Use a hand-held blender to emulsify the warm cream and white chocolate, pouring the cream in a steady stream into the chocolate. Initially, the ganache will split but keep adding the cream and have faith that it will emulsify again. Blend until smooth and glossy. Taste and add a pinch of sea salt, as required. Cover the surface of the ganache with some baking parchment or cling film (plastic wrap) to prevent a skin forming. Refrigerate for a minimum of

6 hours and ideally for 24 hours. If you are tight for time, instead of refrigerating or freezing the ganache, you can chill it over an ice bath, stirring regularly.

Day three

1. Whisk the ganache in a medium bowl until light – you are looking for soft peaks or the texture of clotted cream. You can return the ganache to the refrigerator to set or use straightaway.
2. Line two baking trays (pans) with baking parchment and set aside. Make weighted parcels with silicone muffin cases and baking beans (pie weights), then set aside.
3. Preheat the oven to 200°C (425°F). While the oven is preheating, press a muffin case filled with baking beans into the centre of each dough square. Lightly egg wash around the edges of each pastry.
4. Place the trays in the oven and reduce the temperature to 190°C (400°F). Bake the pastries for 5 minutes, then turn the oven down to 180°C (390°F) and bake for a further 13 minutes. If your oven has hot spots, rotate the trays halfway through.
5. Remove the pastries from the oven and leave to cool for a few minutes before removing the muffin cases.

To assemble the Danish pastries

1. Spoon a generous tablespoon (25–30 g/0.9 oz) of raspberry jam into the bottom of each pastry cavity.
2. Heat a tablespoon in boiling water and form a rocher of whipped ganache (there are lots of videos online that show how to do this), then place carefully on top of the jam.
3. Heat the spoon again and create a little well by gently pushing the back of the spoon into the ganache. Drizzle a teaspoon of fig leaf oil into the well you have just created.
4. Toss the fresh raspberries in fig leaf oil and gently place on top of the pastries – use about four or five raspberries per pastry. I like to cut one or two raspberries in half to expose the dainty seeds inside.

Kimchi and Coolea Cheese Bear Claws

Makes 6–8 bear claws
Time 2 days with Master recipe

Batch of *Croissant Dough* (see page 25)
280–300 g (9.9–10.6 oz) *Carrot and Spring Onion Kimchi* (see page 210) or shop-bought kimchi
120–140 g (4.2–4.9 oz) Coolea cheese or Gouda, grated
Egg Wash (see page 209)
Hot Sauce (see page 197) or shop-bought hot sauce
Togarashi (see page 213) or shop-bought togarashi

For the Kimchi Béchamel Sauce

50 g (1.8 oz) whole milk
200 g (7 oz) kimchi juice (from a shop-bought jar of kimchi)
45 g (1.6 oz) unsalted butter
45 g (1.6 oz) plain (all-purpose) flour
2 g (½ teaspoon) Korean chilli (hot pepper) flakes
50 g (1.8 oz) Coolea cheese or Gouda, grated
12 g (0.4 oz) caster (superfine) sugar
Fine sea salt

Think of the best cheese toastie you've ever had, then imagine it in croissant form. Kimchi is a traditional Korean dish made from salted and fermented cabbage, Korean chilli (hot pepper) flakes and salted fermented shrimp. We make ours from scratch with a lot of Irish grown grated carrot and shredded dillisk seaweed in place of the shrimp, making it vegetarian. You can use shop-bought kimchi instead. Keep the pickle liquid in the jar as it makes the most amazing kimchi béchamel sauce. The same can also be said of hot sauce and togarashi: shop-bought alternatives are perfect and can bought at Asian supermarkets.

Coolea cheese is produced in West Cork. It's sweet, nutty and smooth and melts wonderfully, and is reminiscent of a good-quality Dutch Gouda. You can source it from cheesemongers and supermarket cheese counters across Ireland. It's also available in the UK via Neal's Yard Dairy. You can switch out Coolea for Gouda, or an extra-mature Irish Cheddar also works perfectly.

1. If you are making your own hot sauce or spring onion kimchi, start by fermenting this a week beforehand.
2. Laminate the dough, following the instructions on pages 25–29. Ensure you perform three single folds and that the dough has chilled in the refrigerator for a minimum of 3 hours. While the dough is resting, make the fillings.
3. To make the kimchi béchamel sauce, warm the milk and kimchi juice in a small saucepan over a low heat. The mixture will curdle from the acidity of the juice. Bring to a gentle simmer and then remove from the heat.
4. Melt the butter in a medium saucepan, then add the flour and Korean chilli flakes. Stir continuously until a paste forms – this is called a roux – then cook for 2–3 minutes.
5. Add the kimchi milk to the roux in three stages, whisking as you do so until you have a smooth, silky sauce. Cook over a low heat for 3–4 minutes until thick. Whisk in the Coolea cheese (or Gouda) and season with the sugar and salt to taste. Set aside. The béchamel sauce can be stored in an airtight container for up to a week.
6. While the dough is resting, remove the kimchi from the refrigerator and drain it using a sieve (fine-mesh strainer) over a small bowl or container, using your hands to squeeze out any excess moisture. Transfer the béchamel sauce to a piping (pastry) bag. Line two baking trays (pans) with baking parchment and set aside.
7. Follow steps 3 and 4 on page 31 for instructions on rolling out the croissant dough. The rectangle of dough should be 18 cm (7 in) wide and 4 mm (¼ in) thick after rolling, then 15 cm (6 in) wide after trimming down.
8. Cut out six to eight smaller rectangles, so each one is 9 cm (3½ in) wide and 15 cm (6 in) long.
9. Pipe two parallel lines of béchamel sauce onto the top two thirds of the pastry. Squeeze out the kimchi again to be sure you've removed as much moisture as possible and place a pile in the

centre of the sauce – about 35 g (1.2 oz) per pastry. Next, top with the grated Coolea cheese or Gouda – you are aiming for 15–20 g (0.5–0.7 oz) of cheese in each pastry.

10 Roll the pastries into a Swiss-roll (jelly-roll) shape, tucking the béchamel sauce, kimchi and cheese tightly inside. With the closed side of the pastry facing you, cut two slits a third of the way into the pastry to create the toes of the claws.

11 Place three or four pastries on each baking tray and lightly brush with the egg wash. Place the trays in the oven, but do not turn it on. Leave to prove until inflated, soft and delicate. This can take 1½–2 hours. Once proved, remove from the oven.

12 Preheat the oven to 200°C (425°F) and lightly egg wash each pastry again. Place the trays in the oven and reduce the temperature to 190°C (400°F). Bake the pastries for 5 minutes, then turn the oven down to 180°C (390°F) and bake for a further 13 minutes. If your oven has hot spots, rotate the trays halfway through.

13 Remove the bear claws from the oven, brush liberally with hot sauce and sprinkle the top of each one with some togarashi.

14 Enjoy the bear claws warm from the oven. We like to cut them in half and sandwich them with a soft, gooey fried egg.

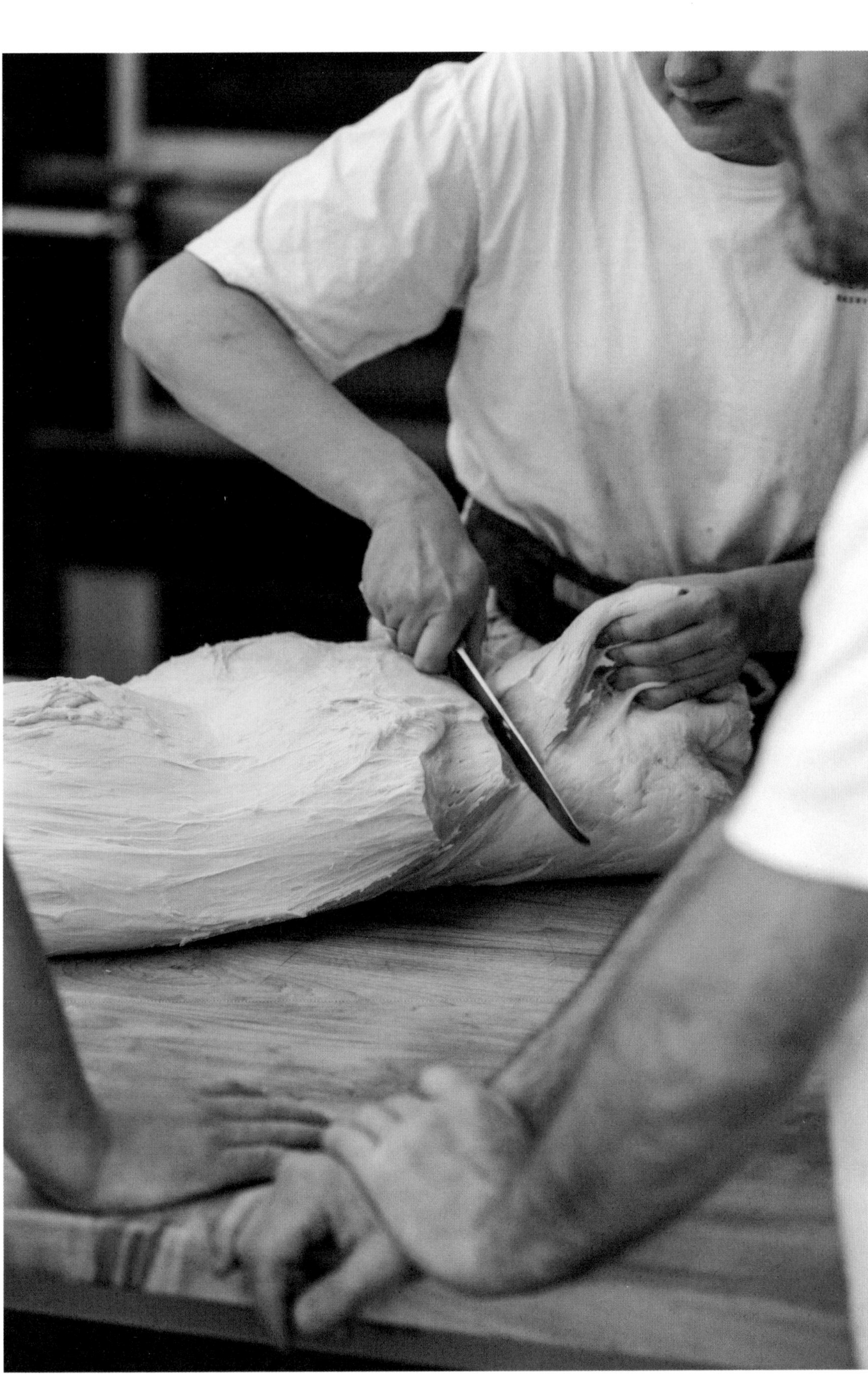

Everything Croissants

Makes 8 croissants
Time 2 days with Master recipe

Batch of *Croissant Dough* (see page 25)
Everything Seed Mix (see page 212) or everything bagel seasoning (available online)
Brown Butter (see page 209)
Melted unsalted butter, for greasing
Finely chopped chives, to garnish

For the Cream Cheese Filling

600 g	(1 lb 5 oz) *Labneh* (see page 212) or shop-bought cream cheese
135 g	(4.7 oz) cream
105 g	(3.7 oz) red onion (about 1 medium onion), finely diced

An 'everything bagel' is an immortal American classic – a thick-crusted bagel rolled in poppy and sesame seeds and seasoned with salt, garlic powder and onion powder. Traditionalists enjoy it smeared with cream cheese. Inspired by takeout bagels from Wise Sons Jewish Delicatessen in San Francisco, we carried those iconic flavours into our croissant menu at Scéal.

1. If you are making your own labneh, start this on the same day you are laminating the croissants. Laminate the dough, following the instructions on pages 25 –29. Ensure you perform three single folds and that the dough has chilled in the refrigerator for a minimum of 3 hours.
2. First, make the filling. Fold the strained labneh (or shop-bought cream cheese), cream and red onion together in a bowl. Transfer to a piping (pastry) bag fitted with a large, star-shaped nozzle (tip). The filling can be stored in the refrigerator for up to a week.
3. Line two baking trays (pans) with baking parchment and set aside. Grease eight 10 cm (4 in) perforated ring moulds with butter.
4. Follow steps 3 and 4 on page 31 for instructions on rolling out the croissant dough. The rectangle of dough should be 21 cm (8¼ in) wide and 5 mm (¼ in) thick after rolling, then 20 cm (8 in) wide after trimming down.
5. Cut out eight squares, so each one measures 10 x 10 cm (4 x 4 in). Each pastry should weigh 90–100 g (3.2–3.5 oz).
6. Pipe 15 g (0.5 oz) of cream cheese filling into the centre of each square. Gather each corner of the square and pin it into the centre of the pastry, creating a small parcel. Next, tip the everything seed mix or everything bagel seasoning onto a small tray. Roll each parcel base and sides in the seed mix.
7. Place each parcel inside a ring mould, allowing four per baking tray. Place the trays in the oven, but do not turn it on. Leave to prove until inflated, soft and delicate. This can take 1½–2 hours. Once proved, they will expand to the edges of the moulds and be puffy and light. Remove from the oven before preheating.
8. Preheat the oven to 200°C (425°F). Pinch in the centres of the croissants if they have popped up during the proving stage. Place the baking trays in the oven and reduce the temperature to 190°C (400°F). Bake the pastries for 5 minutes, then turn the oven down to 180°C (390°F) and bake for a further 13–15 minutes. If your oven has hot spots, rotate the trays halfway through.
9. While the croissants are still hot, remove from the moulds, as they can stick once cooled. Brush with melted brown butter and leave to cool completely. Pipe the top of each pastry with a rosette of cream cheese filling and sprinkle with chives.

PASTRY

Master Recipe:
Spelt Flaky Pastry

Makes 1 x 30 cm (12 in) galette or 4 individual galettes
Time 2 days

75 g	(2.7 oz) iced water
150 g	(5.3 oz) cold unsalted butter
115 g	(4.1 oz) plain (all-purpose) flour, plus extra for dusting
115 g	(4 .1 oz) finely milled spelt flour
3 g	(¾ teaspoon) fine sea salt

I trained as a baker in the US and I'm guilty of using American terminology for the recipes I learned, which is why I refer to what we know as rough puff as flaky pastry. Flaky is a variation of puff pastry, requiring less time and fewer folds. It is a great recipe for beginners to start with before moving on to more complex doughs such as puff pastry, inverted puff or croissant dough.

Once baked, this pastry is incredibly light, crisp and delicate. Another perk of having this recipe in your repertoire is its versatility. We use it for *Seasonal Fruit Galettes* (see page 62), *Whiskey Mince Pies* (see page 177) and *Pork, Apple and Mustard Sausage Rolls* (see page 182). If you can't get your hands on finely milled spelt flour, you could use plain (all-purpose) flour, emmer or einkorn instead. The latter two will impart a delicate nutty, buttery flavour to the pastry.

RECIPE CONTINUED OVERLEAF

Day one

1 Weigh the water and set aside in the refrigerator or freezer to chill.
2 Cut the butter into 5 cm (2 in) cubes and chill.
3 Weigh the flours and salt into the bowl of a stand mixer fitted with the paddle attachment. Add the chilled butter.
4 Turn the mixer to a low speed. Allow the flour to coat the butter pieces. Mix for 1–2 minutes while watching the butter – it should form large, flat, irregular pieces and have a sandy texture.
5 Begin adding the water. Slowly pour one third of the water into the pastry mixture, allowing it to incorporate. Then add another third. At this stage, the pastry may come together as a rough cohesive ball around the paddle attachment.
6 Use your judgement here: add a splash more water if the mixture needs it. You want to just bring the pastry together, while also ensuring there is enough water to hydrate the flour. The pastry shouldn't be sticky or tacky to the touch.
7 Tip the pastry onto a lightly floured surface, pressing it together with your hands. Form a flat, rough rectangle. Cover tightly with cling film (plastic wrap) or a beeswax wrap. Push out any air pockets. Place in the refrigerator to chill for a minimum of 12 hours and ideally 24 hours.

DAY TWO (STEP 3)

PERFORMING A SINGLE FOLD

Day two

1 The aim of the game now is to move fast, so the butter doesn't heat up or melt.
2 Take the pastry out of the refrigerator and place on a lightly floured surface. You need space for this process – I use my kitchen table.
3 Roll the pastry into a large rectangle, roughly 45 x 30 cm (18 x 12 in) and 4–5 mm (¼ in) thick. Roll the pastry away from you in long, even rolls. Take one edge of the pastry and fold it in half along the length. Then take the remaining edge and fold it on top – as if you are folding a letter to put in an envelope. This is called a single fold.
4 At this stage, the piece of pastry will be irregular in shape and rough in appearance. Don't fret, as it'll become more uniform as you perform more folds.
5 Turn the pastry 90 degrees. Lightly flour the work surface again, if necessary. Roll the dough into another rough rectangle – 45 x 30 cm (18 x 12 in) and 4–5mm (¼ in) thick. As before, take one edge and fold it halfway along the length of the pastry. Take the remaining edge and fold it over the bottom layer. This is two single folds completed.
6 Wrap the pastry in cling film or a beeswax wrap and chill in the refrigerator for 1 hour. At this point, you will notice that the butter is still visible in large streaks and smears.
7 Remove the pastry from the refrigerator and place on a lightly floured surface. Make sure the pastry is rotated 90 degrees. Repeat steps 3 and 5. Once the pastry is rolled and folded, you will have successfully completed single folds three and four. Cover the pastry tightly and chill for 1 hour. Alternatively, keep the pastry in the freezer until you are ready to bake. Ensure it is tightly sealed in cling film to avoid freezer burn. Defrost the pastry in the refrigerator – this can take from 6–12 hours – and do not return the dough to the freezer once defrosted.

DAY TWO (STEP 5)

PERFORMING THE SECOND SINGLE FOLD

Seasonal Fruit Galettes

Makes 1 large galette or
4 individual galettes
Time 2 days with Master recipe

Large (29 cm/11½ in diameter)
You will need 400 g (14.1 oz) of fruit

Individual (15.5 cm/6 in diameter)
You will need 100 g (3.5 oz) of fruit for each individual galette

---

Batch of *Spelt Flaky Pastry* (see page 58)

1	large (extra-large) egg, beaten
25–40 g	(0.9–1.4 oz) Demerara sugar

For Rhubarb

400 g	(14.1 oz) rhubarb, cut into 2 cm (¾ in) pieces
15 g	(0.5 oz) caster (superfine) sugar
3 g	(¾ teaspoon) cornflour (cornstarch)

For Apple

400 g	(14.1 oz) eating (dessert apples, core removed and thinly sliced
10 g	(0.4 oz) caster (superfine) sugar
3 g	(¾ teaspoon) cornflour (cornstarch)

For Strawberry/Blackberry/Gooseberry/Loganberry/Tayberry

400 g	(14.1 oz) fruit, halved or quartered
10 g	(0.4 oz) caster (superfine) sugar
3 g	(¾ teaspoon) cornflour (cornstarch)

For Peach/Nectarine/Apricot/Plum/Cherry

400 g	(14.1 oz) fruit, halved, stoned and thinly sliced
10 g	(0.4 oz) caster (superfine) sugar
3 g	(¾ teaspoon) cornflour (cornstarch)

For me, galettes are elegant and unpretentious. It takes confidence to serve up a charming dessert composed of so few ingredients. I prefer to use a single variety of fruit when baking galettes. It's a wonderful way to showcase one fruit's character and complexity. Please use your own creativity and what you love to eat.

1. Preheat the oven to 190°C (400°F).
2. Put the fruit into a large mixing bowl along with the sugar and cornflour. Toss with your hands to evenly coat the fruit pieces. The purpose of the cornflour is to absorb the liquid from the fruit and create its own sauce within the galette. It also prevents the dreaded soggy bottom. Set aside while you roll out the pastry.
3. Remove the pastry from the refrigerator and lightly flour the work surface. Roll into a square, 3–4 mm (¼ in) thick. For a large galette, you are aiming for a diameter of 29 cm (11½ in), which is an average dinner plate. For individual galettes, the diameter should be 15.5 cm (6 in), which is a small side plate. Cut out your disc(s). Put the pastry in the refrigerator to relax for 10 minutes.
4. Remove the pastry disc(s) from the refrigerator and place on a baking sheet lined with baking parchment.
5. Cut five small slits around the perimeter of the disc(s), about 2 cm (¾ in) long. Place the fruit in the centre of the pastry disc(s) and fold the five sides up, encasing the fruit and holding it in place.
6. Brush the edges of the galette(s) with the beaten egg and sprinkle liberally with Demerara sugar.
7. Bake in the oven for 10 minutes, then reduce the temperature to 180°C (390°F). For small galettes, bake for a further 25 minutes. For a large galette, bake for a further 35 minutes. If your oven has hot spots, rotate the baking sheet halfway through.
8. Serve the fruit galette(s) warm with lightly whipped cream or vanilla ice cream.

Notes on Choux Pastry

Choux is incredibly versatile. It can be piped into an array of shapes and sizes to create different pastries and desserts. Over the years, we have baked choux au craquelin, éclairs, profiteroles and Paris-Brest. Once baked, choux is a wonderful vessel for carrying various fillings and flavours. I love to play around with different infusions in creams, jams (jellies) and compotes, pralines and pastes when developing new choux pastries for our menu in the bakery. Many people are intimidated by baking choux at home. Please don't be. The two basic techniques required – cooking a roux and baking – you have more than likely used before.

Choux is cooked in two steps. First, you cook the choux in a saucepan on the hob (stovetop) by making a roux to gelatinise the starch in the flour. Next, when baking the choux, those starches expand and then set to form the crust. The milk, water and egg create steam, which evaporates.

Making choux paste

Over the following pages, I share our choux pastry recipe with you – commonly called *pâte à choux* – and a couple of variations in size and piping techniques. The base recipe and baking technique are the same. Here are some tips on making choux paste:

- The absorption of the quantity of egg into the choux paste will vary every time you make choux. This is due to the evaporation of the liquid in the roux and the absorption capabilities of the flour. For the choux paste used in the recipes in this book, on average, I didn't use 15 g (0.5 oz) of egg. You might find you need to add more egg to achieve the right consistency.
- Every bag and brand of flour is different – from how it was milled, to its freshness, to how it was stored. This can also influence how much of the egg is absorbed.
- Choux paste should have a glossy, smooth and thick consistency. It should create a 'V' or 'beak' on your spatula or paddle attachment and then drop off.
- I use a reusable piping (pastry) bag when piping choux. Air pockets in the piping bag will translate as air bubbles in the choux, so try your best to push out any large air pockets before you start piping.
- If you're not happy with your piping, try again. Choux paste can be reworked and re-piped.
- I don't add sugar to choux paste. Craquelin crust adds sweetness, as do the filling options.
- You can scale up the choux paste recipe to make larger batches. You can also reduce it, but I wouldn't go any further than half the quantities given here.

Craquelin crust

Craquelin dough is a simple mixture of butter, sugar and flour. It is a pastry chef's trick that is greater than the sum of its parts. If you were to bake craquelin on its own, it would be similar to a tuile or snap biscuit (cookie). When baked on top of choux paste, it transforms choux into uniform, elegant pastries. It will disguise any lumps or mistakes in your piping skills as it drapes over the crust. It melts over the top of choux, adding a great texture and uniform shape. Icing (confectioners') sugar and cocoa (unsweetened chocolate) powder cling to it in an elegant way for a refined finish.

Baker's notes

- Craquelin dough will keep in the refrigerator for a week. It can also be stored in the freezer for up to two months.
- You can re-roll craquelin dough. Once you have cut the desired shapes, gather the remaining dough, chill it and re-roll as needed.

Choux au Craquelin Buns

Makes 10–12 choux buns
Time 2–3 days

---

200 g (7 oz) *Blackcurrant Jam* (see page 195) or shop-bought blackcurrant jam (jelly)
Icing (confectioners') sugar, for dusting

For the Blackcurrant Leaf Crémeux

115 g	(4.1 oz) cream, plus extra to top up
15 g	(0.5 oz) blackcurrant leaves
115 g	(4.1 oz) whole milk
10 g	(0.4 oz) caster (superfine) sugar
1	sheet of gelatine
45 g	(1.6 oz) egg yolk (about 2 UK medium/ US large eggs)
75 g	(2.7 oz) white chocolate

For the Craquelin Crust

50 g	(1.8 oz) unsalted butter (at room temperature)
50 g	(1.8 oz) caster (superfine) sugar
50 g	(1.8 oz) plain (all-purpose) flour

Generous pinch of fine sea salt

For the Choux Paste

125 g	(4.4 oz) water
125 g	(4.4 oz) whole milk
3.5 g	(¾ teaspoon) fine sea salt
115 g	(4.1 oz) unsalted butter
140 g	(4.9 oz) strong white bread flour (I use Dove's Farm Organic Flour)
200 g	(7 oz) egg (about 4 UK medium/US large eggs)

Choux au craquelin buns are the perfect vessel for carrying flavours and fillings. Here I have used blackcurrant leaf to infuse my crémeux, mirroring the flavour of the blackcurrant jam (jelly). I use my homemade *Blackcurrant Jam* (see page 195), but you can also use shop-bought jam. Blackcurrant leaves contain essential oils reminiscent of the berry: sweet, earthy and floral. The crémeux recipe is adaptable – you can leave it plain with vanilla pods (beans) or replace the blackcurrant leaves with lemon verbena, fig leaves, elderflower blossom, sweet woodruff, whole spices, tea leaves or citrus rind. The jam can also be swapped out for another favourite or something from your larder.

Day one

1 To make the blackcurrant leaf crémeux, heat the cream in a small saucepan until just below boiling point. Remove from the heat, then add the blackcurrant leaves (or your choice of flavouring) to the cream and leave to infuse for 2 hours at room temperature, then transfer to the refrigerator once cool to infuse for a further 22 hours.

Day two

1 Strain the cream, squeeze out the leaves and weigh the cream again. If necessary, top up with fresh cream to a total of 115 g (4 oz). The leaves will have absorbed some of the cream during infusion.
2 Put the cream, milk and sugar into a small saucepan and bring to the boil. At the same time, bloom the gelatine in some cold water.
3 Whisk the egg yolks and pour over the hot cream mixture. Return to the heat and cook until the mixture reaches 82°C (180°F). Meanwhile, squeeze out the excess water from the bloomed gelatine. Remove from the heat and whisk in the bloomed gelatine. Set aside for a couple of minutes.
4 Melt the white chocolate in a bain-marie or in a bowl in the microwave. Using a hand-held blender, gradually pour the hot custard into the melted chocolate and emulsify until smooth and glossy. Pour into an airtight container or clean bowl and chill in the refrigerator for at least 6 hours.
5 To make the craquelin crust, combine everything in a mixing bowl (or use the paddle attachment in the bowl of a stand mixer). You are not looking to incorporate any air or cream into the mixture. Bring together to form a smooth dough. Wrap in cling film (plastic wrap) or baking parchment and chill in the refrigerator for a minimum of 2 hours and ideally for 24 hours.

Day three

1 To make the choux paste, add the water, milk, salt and butter to a medium saucepan and bring to a boil. The butter needs to be fully melted before you move on to the next step.
2 Add the flour to the boiling liquid and turn the heat down to low.

Using a wooden spoon or a sturdy spatula, beat the flour into the liquid, mixing continuously until a paste forms. Cook out the roux paste for 2 minutes – the paste will clean the edges of the saucepan and begin to stick to the base.

3 Transfer the paste to a clean bowl, or if you are using a stand mixer, the bowl with the paddle attachment. Mix slowly for 2 minutes to allow the steam to evaporate and the paste to cool down.

4 Whisk the eggs with a fork until uniform. Add the eggs in parts to the choux paste. If you are doing this by hand or in the mixer, wait until the egg is fully incorporated before you add the next amount, using about 25 g (0.9 oz) at a time. Take your time here: wait until the egg is fully absorbed before adding the next amount. Hold back a small amount of egg (about 25 g/0.9 oz) and check the consistency. The choux should be thick but not too thick. It should fall off your spatula (or paddle attachment), look shiny and feel super smooth.

5 The choux is now ready to use for baking. Or you can store it in the refrigerator at this point in an airtight container for up to three days.

6 Transfer the choux paste to a piping bag. Work the choux paste down the piping bag with the side of your hand or a spatula, squeezing out any air pockets as you go.

7 Preheat the oven to 220°C (475°F).

8 While the oven is preheating, whip the crémeux by hand or in a stand mixer until it is the texture of whipped cream. Transfer to a piping (pastry) bag fitted with a star-shaped nozzle (tip) and return to the refrigerator.

9 Now cut the craquelin crust. Remove the dough from the refrigerator and peel back the top layer of baking parchment. Cut out 12 discs, 5 cm (2 in) in diameter. If you don't have enough discs, gather up the excess dough, re-roll it, then chill and cut again. Set aside the discs.

10 Line two baking trays (pans) with baking parchment. Draw 12 circles over the two trays, ensuring they are 5 cm (2 in) in diameter. Aim for a 4–5 cm (1.5–2 in) gap between the circles. These will act as your guide for piping out the choux paste.

11 Holding the piping bag vertically, directly above the baking tray, begin to apply even pressure. Pipe even rounds within your marked lines, weighing about 45–50 g (1.6–1.8 oz) each. Place a craquelin crust disc on top of each piped bun.

12 Place the baking trays in the oven and immediately reduce the heat to 190°C (400°F). Bake for 15 minutes, then turn the heat down to 160°C (350°F) and bake for a further 10–15 minutes. The choux should be well baked, light and crisp. Remove from the oven and leave to cool completely on a wire rack before filling.

13 Use a serrated knife to carefully cut open one of the choux buns – two-thirds base to one-third top. Spoon about 15 g (0.5 oz) of blackcurrant jam into the bottom of the bun. Holding the piping bag vertically, pipe a little of the whipped crémeux on top of the jam, then pipe a rosette around the edge. Place the lid of the bun on top. Repeat for all the choux buns.

14 Dust the choux buns with icing sugar and enjoy.

Éclairs with Milk Chocolate and Olive Oil

Makes 12 éclairs
Time 2 days

Burned Honey Chocolate Glaze (see page 196)
Cocoa nibs, to garnish

For the Olive Oil Namelaka

1	sheet of gelatine
50 g	(1.8 oz) whole milk
85 g	(3 oz) milk chocolate
2 g	(½ teaspoon) coconut oil
100 g	(3.5 oz) cream
20 g	(0.7 oz) extra-virgin olive oil

Pinch of flaky sea salt

For the Chocolate Craquelin Crust

50 g	(1.8 oz) unsalted butter (at room temperature)
50 g	(1.8 oz) caster (superfine) sugar
35 g	(1.2 oz) plain (all-purpose) flour
15 g	(0.5 oz) cocoa (unsweetened chocolate) powder

Generous pinch of fine sea salt

For the Choux Paste

125 g	(4.4 oz) water
125 g	(4.4 oz) whole milk
3.5 g	(¾ teaspoon) fine sea salt
112 g	(4 oz) butter
137 g	(4.8 oz) strong white bread flour
200 g	(7 oz) egg (about 4 UK medium/US large eggs)

Namelaka means 'smooth' or 'creamy' in Japanese. I first learned this technique for a super-creamy ganache filling while working in Craftsman and Wolves in San Francisco. It is a silky-smooth emulsion of milk, cream and chocolate set with gelatine that makes a wonderful carrier for infusions. The chocolate can be switched out for white or dark. Use a good-quality extra virgin olive oil for this recipe. I would lean towards one that has a fruity rather than peppery, spicy finish.

Day one

1 First, make the olive oil namelaka. Bloom the gelatine in cold water. At the same time, heat the milk to 65–70°C (149–158°F). You don't want the milk to boil. This can be done in the microwave or in a small saucepan. Add the bloomed gelatine to the milk and whisk to incorporate and dissolve the gelatine.
2 Melt the chocolate and coconut oil together in a small bowl over a saucepan of simmering water. Using a hand-held blender, emulsify the melted chocolate by pouring the milk into the chocolate. The emulsion will crack on you, but don't panic! Keep blending until all the milk has been added. Next, add the cream and olive oil in a steady stream and blend until silky smooth.
3 Taste the namelaka and add a pinch of sea salt. Pour into an airtight container or small bowl and keep in the refrigerator – ideally for 24 hours to allow the chocolate to set and the gelatine to firm up.
4 To make the chocolate craquelin crust, combine everything in a mixing bowl (or in a stand mixer fitted with the paddle attachment). Bring together to form a smooth dough. Wrap in cling film (plastic wrap) or baking parchment and chill in the refrigerator for a minimum of 2 hours, or ideally for 24 hours.

Day two

1 Transfer the namelaka to a piping (pastry) bag fitted with a round nozzle (tip). Return to the refrigerator until you are ready to fill the éclairs. The filling will keep for four days. It doesn't freeze well.
2 Roll the craquelin dough out between two sheets of baking parchment to 3–4 mm (¼ in) thick. Return to the refrigerator to firm up.
3 To make the choux paste, put the water, milk, salt and butter into a medium saucepan and bring to the boil. The butter must be fully melted before you move on to the next step.
4 Add the flour to the boiling liquid and turn the heat down to low. Using a wooden spoon or a sturdy spatula, beat the flour into the liquid, mixing continuously until a paste forms. Cook out the roux paste for 2 minutes – the paste will clean the edges of the saucepan and begin to stick to the base.
5 Transfer the paste to a clean bowl or a stand mixer fitted with the paddle attachment. Mix slowly for 2 minutes to allow the steam to evaporate and the paste to cool down.

6. Whisk the eggs with a fork until uniform. Add about 25 (0.9 oz) to the choux paste and beat in. Continue gradually adding the eggs, making sure they are fully incorporated before adding more. When you have about 25 g (0.9 oz) of egg left,check the consistency. The choux should be thick but not too thick. It should fall off your spatula (or paddle attachment), look shiny and feel super smooth. If it isn't, add the remaining egg.
7. The choux is now ready to use for baking, or you can store it in the refrigerator in an airtight container for up to 3 days.
8. Transfer the choux paste to a piping bag. Work the choux paste down the piping bag with the side of your hand or a spatula, squeezing out any air pockets as you go. Next, transfer the choux paste to a piping bag with a large, star-shaped nozzle. Again, work the choux paste down the piping bag, squeezing out any air pockets as before.
9. Preheat the oven to 220°C (475°F).
10. While the oven is preheating, cut the craquelin crust. Remove the dough from the refrigerator and peel back the top layer of baking parchment. Cut the crust into 10 x 1.5 cm (4 x ½ in) rectangles. You will need to cut out 12 strips. If you don't have enough strips, gather up the excess dough, re-roll it, then chill and cut again. Set aside.
11. Line two baking trays (pans) with baking parchment. Draw six 12 cm (5 in) lines on each sheet of baking parchment. You should have 12 lines in total.
12. Hold the piping bag at a 45-degree angle to the baking tray. Using an even pressure, pipe a straight line of choux paste along each of your marked-out lines. Pipe as evenly and straight as you can. The éclairs should weigh about 25 g (0.9 oz) each. Ensure there is a 4 cm (1½ in) gap between each piped éclair because they will expand as they bake.
13. Place the craquelin crusts on top of each éclair.
14. Place both baking trays in the oven and immediately reduce the heat to 190°C (400°F). Bake for 15 minutes, then turn the temperature down to 160°C (350°F) and continue baking for a further 10 minutes. The éclairs should be light and crisp. Keep an eye on their colour as they can darken quickly due to the cocoa powder in the crust. Remove the éclairs from the oven and allow to cool completely on a wire rack before filling them.
15. Cut the éclairs in half lengthways. Pipe an even line of olive oil namelaka along the centre of each éclair. You are aiming for 25 g (1 oz) in each one. Gently press the top of the éclair onto the filling to ensure it is firmly in place for the glazing step. Repeat for all the éclairs. Place in the refrigerator to chill for 5–10 minutes.
16. While the éclairs are chilling, melt the burned honey chocolate glaze until it is shiny, smooth and runny. Have a clean baking tray lined with baking parchment prepared.
17. Dip the top half of each éclair in the glaze, gently shake off the excess and place on the baking tray. Sprinkle the éclairs with cocoa nibs. These are best enjoyed within a couple of hours of filling.

Apple Crumble Tart with Bay Leaf Custard

Makes 1 x 24 cm (9½ in) tart
Time 3 hours 30 minutes

For the Sweet Pastry

165 g (5.8 oz) unsalted butter
75 g (2.7 oz) icing (confectioners') sugar
Zest of 1 lemon
4 g (1 teaspoon) fine sea salt
45 g (1.6 oz) egg yolk (about 3 UK medium/US large eggs)
265 g (9.3 oz) plain (all-purpose) flour

For the Apple Compote

5 Bramley (cooking) apples (about 1 kg/2 lb 4 oz before peeling and coring)
100 g (3.5 oz) caster (superfine) sugar
Zest of ½ lemon
30 g (1 oz) unsalted butter

For the Oat Crumble

100 g (3.5 oz) plain (all-purpose) flour
100 g (3.5 oz) unsalted butter
50 g (1.8 oz) caster (superfine) sugar
50 g (1.8 oz) Demerara sugar
50 g (1.8 oz) rolled oats
50 g (1.8 oz) ground almonds (almond meal)
5 g (1 teaspoon) fine sea salt

For the Bay Leaf Custard

250 g (8.8 oz) cream
4 bay leaves
60 g (2 oz) egg yolk (about 3 UK medium/US large eggs)
50 g (1.8 oz) caster (superfine) sugar

There are two mature Bramley (cooking) apple trees in my parents' back garden. They were planted before they bought our family home 40 years ago. Come late autumn, my dad chooses a date to start picking the apples – usually before the first stormy night is forecast, so he doesn't lose the pickings to windfalls. Each year while I was growing up, Mimi and my mum creatively tried to use every apple. Jars of apple and sultana (golden raisin) chutney, clear glistening pots of apple jelly, Christmas puddings, mincemeat and apple butter were in heavy rotation every year. We were also guaranteed a crumble being baked every weekend.

This tart is a refined version of my childhood crumble. The sweet pastry recipe is rich and short in texture, and a resourceful one to use for blind-baked tart cases (shells) or fresh fruit tarts. The compote has two different-sized apple pieces for texture and acidity. The oat crumble topping is very versatile. We use it in our *Whiskey Mince Pies* (see page 177). The custard is a rich, thick, luscious pouring custard. If bay leaf is too pungent for you, replace the bay with one vanilla pod (bean) or a stick of cinnamon.

1 To make the sweet pastry, use an electric hand mixer or stand mixer fitted with the paddle attachment to cream together the butter, sugar, lemon zest and salt until pale.
2 Add the egg yolks one at a time, scraping down the sides of the bowl between each addition.
3 Add the flour to the bowl in two stages, keeping the speed on low. Don't overmix the dough at this point. Bring the dough together to form a ball, then press firmly into a square and cover tightly with cling film (plastic wrap). Store in the refrigerator for a minimum of one hour and up to 3 days.
4 To make the apple compote, prepare the apple in two ways. First wash, peel and core all the apples (you should have around 800 g/ 1 lb 12 oz of apple). Then chop 400 g (14.1 oz) of the apple into rough 2 cm (¾ cm) cubes and the remaining 400 g (14.1 oz) into smaller 1 cm (½ in) cubes.
5 Add the larger apple cubes, sugar and lemon zest to a medium saucepan. Cook over a medium heat for 8 minutes. The compote will have a smooth texture with some larger pieces of apple through it. Fold through the butter and the smaller apple cubes. Store in an airtight container and leave to cool before placing in the refrigerator where it will keep for 5 days.
6 To make the oat crumble, combine all the ingredients in a stand mixer fitted with the paddle attachment. Bring together until the mixture has the texture of wet sand – about 5 minutes on a slow speed. Alternatively, rub the butter into the dry ingredients with your hands and a light touch. Keep the oat crumble in the refrigerator until you are ready to bake the tart.
7 Take the chilled sweet pastry out of the refrigerator. Roll out between two sheets of baking parchment or two silicone baking

mats. The pastry should be 3–4 mm (¼ in) thick and approximately 36 cm (14 in) in diameter. This will be enough to cover the base and sides of a 24 cm (9½ in) tart tin (pan) and the sides.

8. Put the rolled-out pastry in the refrigerator on a baking tray (pan) lined with baking parchment to chill and relax for 15 minutes.
9. Remove the pastry from the refrigerator and lay it carefully over the tart tin. Press the pastry into the sides and bottom of the tin. This pastry has a high portion of fat, so it will soften quickly at room temperature. If the pastry is getting too soft to handle, pop it back in the refrigerator or even the freezer if you have space. Trim any excess pastry from around the rim of the tin with a sharp knife. You can use the trimmed pastry bits to patch any holes on the bottom or sides. Chill the pastry again for 10–15 minutes – the length of time it will take for the oven to preheat.
10. Preheat the oven to 170°C (375°F). Remove the pastry-lined tart tin from the refrigerator. Spread the apple compote over the bottom of the pastry in an even layer. Scatter the crumble over the top. I like to squeeze little clusters in my hands for added texture.
11. Bake the tart on the middle shelf of the oven for 45 minutes. Check halfway through – if your oven has hot spots, rotate the tart tin if necessary. Once the tart is golden and evenly baked, remove from the oven and leave to cool.
12. While the tart is baking, prepare the bay leaf custard. Heat the cream and bay leaves together in a small, heavy-based saucepan. Bring to just below boiling point – the surface of the cream will be steaming.
13. While the cream is heating, whisk together the egg yolks and sugar until smooth and lightly aerated (about 30–60 seconds of whisking). Don't allow the egg yolks and sugar to sit together as the sugar will begin to cure the yolks, hardening the outside layer and creating flecks of yolk in the custard.
14. Slowly pour half the hot cream over the egg mixture, whisking continuously. Over a low heat, gradually pour the tempered eggs back into the remaining cream. Switch to a rubber spatula. Continue to cook the custard until it reaches 82°C (180°F) or coats the back of the spatula. Strain through a fine sieve (strainer) to remove the bay leaf and any lumps.
15. Serve the apple crumble tart cold with a generous helping of the bay leaf custard.

Mimi's Best-ever Bakewell Tart

Makes 1 x 20–22 cm (8–8½ in) tart
Time 2 days

150 g	(5.3 oz) *Raspberry Jam* (see page 194) or shop-bought raspberry jam (jelly)
25 g	(0.9 oz) flaked (slivered) almonds

For the Shortcrust Pastry

240 g	(8.5 oz) plain (all-purpose) flour, plus extra for dusting
5 g	(1 teaspoon) fine sea salt
120 g	(4.2 oz) cold unsalted butter, cut into cubes
2	large (extra-large) egg yolks
30 g	(1 oz) full-fat yoghurt

For the Frangipane

85 g	(3 oz) unsalted butter (at room temperature)
85 g	(3 oz) caster (superfine) sugar
2	large eggs (at room temperature)
60 g	(2 oz) plain (all-purpose) flour
115 g	(4.1 oz) ground almonds (almond meal)
2 g	(½ teaspoon) fine sea salt

Baker's note

The frangipane can be made in advance. If you are getting ahead, it can be stored in an airtight container in the refrigerator for up to a week. Take out of the refrigerator to come to room temperature when you are ready to bake.

Throughout this book, you will come across mentions of Mimi. She is the reason I became a pastry chef. From a very young age, she taught me to bake and cook. This is her recipe: a Bakewell tart that is filled with nostalgia. I would have a small slice and a glass of milk as an after-school treat in primary (elementary) school.

Day one

1 To make the shortcrust pastry, combine the flour, salt and butter in a large mixing bowl. Rub the butter into the flour until it resembles fine breadcrumbs. You want the fat to coat the flour particles evenly and for large pieces of butter to be rubbed in.
2 Add the egg yolks and yoghurt and use your hands to mix them into the flour mixture in a circular motion. Bring everything together into a ball, ensuring the sides of the bowl are clean.
3 Flatten the dough into a disc and cover tightly with cling film (plastic wrap) or a beeswax wrap. Squeeze out any air bubbles, as they will make the pastry oxidise. Chill in the refrigerator for 12–24 hours.
4 To make the frangipane, cream the butter and sugar together in a mixing bowl until pale and light in colour. Beat in one of the eggs, scraping down the sides of the bowl and beating until smooth. Add the second egg. The mixture will appear to curdle, but don't worry. You are combining two different fats at two different temperatures and the mix can split. Fold in the flour, ground almonds and salt. Place the frangipane in an airtight container in the refrigerator until you are ready to bake the tart.

Day two

1 Preheat the oven to 170°C (375°F). Remove the shortcrust pastry from the refrigerator and allow to come to room temperature for 5–10 minutes. This will make it easier to roll out and be kinder on your wrists.
2 Roll the pastry out on a lightly floured work surface until it is about 4 mm (¼ in) thick. Lay the pastry over a 20–22 cm (8–8½ in) tart tin (pan) and gently ease it into the corners. If the pastry rips, patch it with a small piece of raw dough. Press the pastry into the bottom and sides of the tin. Using a small, sharp knife, run it along the edge of the tin to trim off the excess dough.
3 Spread an even layer of raspberry jam over the base of the pastry. Using a piping (pastry) bag or an offset spatula, carefully spread the frangipane over the raspberry jam. Smooth the top and sprinkle the flaked almonds around the perimeter of the tart.
4 Place the tart in the centre of the preheated oven and bake for 40 minutes. You may need to rotate the tart halfway through if one side is browning faster than the other. Remove from the oven and let cool completely before serving with softly whipped cream.

MALONE FRUIT FARM We've been using James Malone's fruit for over five years now in the bakery. We first connected when our market stalls were side by side at a weekly farmers' market in South Dublin. The business was first started by Tom and Elizabeth Malone in 1983 as a novel way of keeping their seven children busy during the summer. What started as a project is now a family-run business based in Closh, County Carlow, delivering the best-quality fruits in Ireland in the height of summer.

The first summer of Scéal, I longed for blackcurrants to make jams and compotes. Hit with disappointment, phone call after phone call to all the major fresh produce suppliers in Dublin, I was shocked to hear that all blackcurrants commercially grown in Ireland went into Ribena production. Malone is one of the few berry farmers left in Ireland who grow for the home baker and restaurant and bakery trade in Leinster. The provenance of food and where it has been cultivated is crucial in Malone Fruit Farm's success.

We use our seasonal Danish pastries to highlight and showcase some of Malone's best fruits. The season kicks off with the quintessential flavour of Irish summertime, strawberries, which is Malone's main crop, and in quick succession we have raspberries, gooseberries, loganberries, blackcurrants, redcurrants, blackberries and whitecurrants.

The best-kept secret of Malone Fruit Farm is the tonnes of fruit they pick fresh and freeze for the off-season months. We use James' frozen berries throughout the year in our jars of raspberry and blackcurrant jam (jelly).

Pavlova

Makes 1 large pavlova
Time 3 hours

For the Meringue

100 g	(3.5 oz) egg whites (about 3 UK large/US extra-large eggs)
300 g	(10.6 oz) caster (superfine) sugar
15 g	(0.5 oz) cornflour (cornstarch)
3 g	(¾ teaspoon) fine sea salt
30 g	(1 oz) recently boiled water
7 g	(1½ teaspoons) apple cider vinegar or white vinegar

For the Oven-roasted Plums

10–15	plums, depending on their size
20 g	(0.7 oz) caster (superfine) sugar
Juice of 1 lemon	
50 g	(1.8 oz) Elderflower Syrup (see page 208)

For the Mascarpone Cream

250 g	(8.8 oz) mascarpone
250 g	(8.8 oz) cream
30 g	(1 oz) icing (confectioners') sugar
1	vanilla pod (bean) (optional)

There is no better forkful than sweet marshmallow meringue, lush, rich cream and sour, sharp fruit. Here, I have paired the meringue with tart, floral poached plums and mascarpone cream. But please use this recipe as the seasons change. Think roast strawberries (see page 151) in early summer, plums, damsoms and quince in autumn, and bright citrus in the depths of winter.

1. First, make the meringue. Preheat the oven to 120°C (275°F). Line a baking tray (pan) with baking parchment.
2. Put the egg whites into a stand mixer fitted with the whisk attachment. Whip the egg whites on high speed for 1 minute. The egg whites need to create a foam before you add the sugar.
3. While the egg whites are whipping, combine the sugar, cornflour and salt and whisk together. Mix the cornflour and salt into the sugar with a fork or whisk. With the mixer on high speed, slowly add the sugar mixture to the egg whites, a tablespoon at a time. This will take 2–3 minutes.
4. Add the recently boiled water and vinegar in a steady stream. Continue to whip the meringue on high for a further 4 minutes or until the sugar has dissolved. To check this, rub the meringue between your fingers. Once whipped, you will have a thick, very shiny, glossy meringue.
5. Pile the meringue into the centre of the baking tray. Spread it out with a rubber spatula or offset spatula into a circle approximately 22 cm (9 in) in diameter. I like to create a waved, rippled texture around the edges with a pool in the centre where you can generously mound the filling and fruit. Gently tap the baking tray on the work surface to knock out any big air bubbles.
6. Bake in the oven for 30 minutes, then reduce the temperature to 100°C (250°F) and bake for a further 50–60 minutes. Remove from the oven and leave to cool on the baking tray.
7. Turn the oven up to 180°C (390°F).
8. Wash the plums, pat dry and cut in half. Place the plum halves cut side down in an ovenproof dish, sprinkle over the sugar, lemon juice and elderflower syrup. Cover tightly with kitchen foil and bake for 8 minutes. Remove the foil and roast the plums for a further 8–10 minutes. Check the plums by gently squeezing them between your fingers or with a sharp knife. They should have a gentle give. If they are still firm, return to the oven for a further 1–2 minutes. Take the fruit out of the oven, leave the tray covered in foil and allow to cool completely. The plums and elderflower will create their own gorgeous pink syrup.
9. To make the mascarpone cream, whip together the mascarpone cream, cream, icing sugar and vanilla pod (bean) seeds, if using, until thick and holding soft peaks.
10. Pull the pavlova together an hour or two before serving. Place the meringue shell on a large plate or cake stand. Pile high with the mascarpone cream. Use the spatula to create a puddle in the cream and spoon in the poached plums. Cut generous slices and enjoy!

Basque Cheesecake

Makes 1 x 20 cm (8 in) cheesecake
Time 2 days

750 g	(1 lb 10 oz) labneh (see below) or cream cheese
250 g	(8.8 oz) caster (superfine) sugar
35 g	(1.2 oz) plain (all-purpose) flour
5 g	(1 teaspoon) fine sea salt
300 g	(10.6 oz) eggs (about 7 UK medium/US large eggs), at room temperature
550 g	(19.4 oz) cream

For the Labneh (if making)

1.2 kg	(2 lb 11 oz) full-fat Greek yoghurt
9 g	(½ teaspoon) fine sea salt

I began developing this recipe for family celebrations. Dessert is my go-to contribution to the dinner table. My brother has a wheat intolerance, which means dessert has to be gluten-free. We had leftover labneh in the bakery from our batches of *Everything Croissants* (see page 54). A light bulb dinged in my mind – instead of buying supermarket cream cheese, I would make the cheesecake with our *Labneh* (see page 212). I have never looked back. It is tangy and incredibly creamy. To boot, it also has the moreish flavour of Irish yoghurt that you don't get from shop-bought cream cheese. For a gluten-free option, use cornflour (cornstarch) instead of plain (all-purpose) flour. This is a classic interpretation of the Basque recipe, with no vanilla or lemon zest. If you feel that way inclined, please add these in.

My family enjoys this cheesecake with fresh raspberries, cold pouring cream and *Whiskey Caramel Sauce* (see page 196) or a large spoonful of *Marsala-soaked Prunes* (see page 190).

1. If you're making the labneh, follow the instructions on page 212 but use the quantities list opposite.
2. The next day, prepare the cheesecake. It is important that all ingredients are at room temperature, so remove the labneh and cream from the refrigerator ahead of time. If you store eggs in the refrigerator, also remove these.
3. Preheat the oven to 200°C (425°F). Boil a kettle of water.
4. Line a 20 cm (8 in) cake tin (pan) with baking parchment, using a double layer on the sides. Place on a baking tray (pan).
5. Whisk together the labneh or cream cheese, sugar, flour and salt in a large mixing bowl. You are not looking to incorporate any air during this process.
6. Combine the eggs and cream in a large measuring jug (pitcher) or mixing bowl. Mix together using a hand-held blender.
7. Pour the eggs and cream into the labneh mixture in three stages, making sure to scrape down the bottom of the bowl between each addition of eggs and cream. Then, pour the final mixture through a fine sieve (strainer) into the lined cake tin.
8. Fill a small loaf tin (pan) or ovenproof dish with recently boiled water and place it in the bottom of the oven. Bake the cheesecake for 45 minutes, then check the wobble in the centre (it should be wobbly). It may need another 5 minutes.
9. Remove from the oven and leave to cool and set completely in the tin for 24 hours. Remove from the refrigerator several hours before serving to allow the cheesecake to come up to room temperature.

BREAD

Making a Sourdough Levain

To make a truly good sourdough levain (often referred to as the mother or starter), you need just three things: flour, water and time. It's easy to do, but there are a few things to keep in mind before you begin.

What are wild yeast?

Before you get started, let's talk about wild yeast, which are the key to a sourdough levain. Before we had dried active yeast, we had wild yeast. We still have wild yeast. It lives everywhere – in the air, in a bag of flour, and on the skins and surface of many fruits and vegetables like grapes, pineapple and ginger. Domesticated commercial yeast replaced wild yeast for most baking because it's easier for companies to mass-produce, it's easier for bakers to store and use, and it proves breads and pastries in a fraction of the time.

In contrast, wild yeast can be fussy and finicky. It needs a medium – a sourdough levain – to be useful to bakers. This medium must be constantly maintained and monitored. Wild yeast also like cooler temperatures and acidic environments and work much more slowly to prove bread. So why bother? Because wild yeast is amazing stuff! The flavours are more complex and interesting and the texture is sturdier and more enjoyable to chew.

What is a sourdough levain?

A sourdough levain is how we cultivate the wild yeast in a form that we can use for baking. Simply put, it is a mixture of flour and water that is fermented by wild yeast and lactic acid bacteria. Since wild yeast is present in all flour, the easiest way to make a levain is simply by combining flour and water and letting it sit for several days. You don't need any fancy ingredients to 'capture' the wild yeast or get it going – it's already there in the flour. It's important to note that the yeast will adapt to whatever environment it is in.

With so few ingredients in a sourdough levain, it's essential that those used are of the highest quality. If you live in an area where water quality is compromised, take care to feed your levain with filtered water where possible, as tap water contains chlorine and heavy metals that can damage the beneficial bacteria and yeast in a sourdough levain.

Any flour, provided it's a grain-based and not self-raising, will work to make a sourdough levain. I typically use unbleached organic plain (all-purpose) flour or bread flour.

See *How to Make a Sourdough Levain* on pages 94–99.

Why use an established levain?

The wild fermentation of flour and water will yield beautiful results; however, getting a boost in beneficial bacteria and yeasts from an established levain is always helpful – particularly for first-time sourdough bakers whose technique and knowledge are limited by inexperience. These established sourdough levains – usually sold fresh or dried and powdered – are rich in established bacteria and yeasts, and they will give your sourdough levain a much-needed boost, acting as a sort of insurance policy to ensure your levain begins bubbling away reliably. And it's this level of insurance and reliability that is so helpful to newcomers to sourdough baking. From our experience, your local independent bakery will give you a pinch of sourdough levain for no cost. The more individuals baking at home and understanding the importance of fermentation in our diet, the better.

Master Recipe:
How to Make a Sourdough Levain

Makes 200 g (7 oz)
Time 5–6 days

---

800 g (1 lb 12 oz) of your preferred flour (I like unbleached plain/all-purpose flour)
800 g (1 lb 12 oz) cool filtered water

Levain is the heartbeat of naturally fermented bread. It's a pre-ferment made from wild yeast, bacteria, flour and water, and it provides strength, flavour and rise to your bread. Unlike commercial yeast, which acts quickly, levain develops slowly, allowing complex flavours to emerge, creating a more digestible loaf. It is the natural ferment that gives sourdough its signature texture and sour flavour, and its name.

You will get to know your levain and develop a relationship as she matures. Give her a name once she has grown and you can see what kind of bubbly personality she has. Shane's levain is Geraldine, named after his mother. And, like Shane's mother, she can be a little temperamental and chaotic when he doesn't feed her regularly.

My levain has been fermenting and producing bread babies at our bakery for over eight years now. We have become very close over the years – I even take her home from time to time for holiday feeds and overnight observation.

My best advice for getting the most out of your levain is to be strict, using her only when she is at peak performance – essentially 8 hours after she has been fed a fresh feed of flour and water.

A note on room temperature: the colder the environment, the slower your levain will grow. If the normal daily temperature in your home is 20°C (68°F) or below, I recommend finding a cosy spot for it for the resting period – such as your airing cupboard (we call this a hot press in Ireland) or on top of your refrigerator or coffee machine.

RECIPE CONTINUED OVERLEAF

Day one

Combine the flour and water in a non-reactive container, such as a glass jar, ceramic pot, stainless-steel bowl or food-grade plastic container. Choose a container that will allow the levain to grow in size: one that is 500 ml (17 fl oz) or larger. Mix 100 g (3.5 oz) flour and 100 g (3.5 oz) water together thoroughly, so there are no pockets or lumps of dry flour left. Loosely cover the container to allow air to circulate, place somewhere warm and leave to sit for 24 hours.

Day two

After 24 hours, you will see little to no activity. Discard half of the levain, so 100 g (3.5 oz). Add 100 g (3.5 oz) of flour and 100 g (3.5 oz) of filtered water. Mix thoroughly, cover loosely and leave for a further 24 hours.

Day three

At this stage, you might start to notice some activity – small gas bubbles, a rise and fall in activity and a change in smell that I describe as a sweet, yoghurt-like aroma. At this stage, you will increase the frequency of feedings to two over 24 hours.

Try to space the feeds evenly throughout your day, but don't get too caught up in this, as life and work can come first.

Morning and afternoon
Discard half of the levain, roughly 100 g (3.5 oz). Add 100 g (3.5 oz) of flour and 100 g (3.5 oz) of water. Repeat the mixing/resting process, then leave for 12 hours.

Day four

Morning and afternoon
Discard half of the levain, roughly 100 g (3.5 oz). Add 100 g (3.5 oz) of flour and 100 g (3.5 oz) of water. Repeat the mixing/resting process, then leave for 12 hours.

DAY 1

DAY 3

Day five

Come day five, your levain should smell tangy and sweet like fresh yoghurt but not too sharp like apple cider vinegar. It should be enjoyable to smell. You should notice it doubling in volume after a feed of fresh flour and water. There will be a combination of large bubbles and smaller, finer bubbles.

Morning and afternoon:
Discard half of the levain, roughly 100 g (3.5 oz). Add 100 g (3.5 oz) of flour and 100 g (3.5 oz) of water. Repeat the mixing/resting process, then leave for 12 hours.

Day six

Observe your levain. It should be very active, bubbling and doubling in size after a 12-hour feed of fresh flour and water. The aroma should be sweet and tangy. Pinch a small amount and float it in a glass of water. If it floats on the surface, that means it has trapped loads of air bubbles and is ripe and healthy. If it sinks, I recommend doing another day of feeding and discarding.

Note: removing the old levain from the container is a really important step that's not to be overlooked. If you keep adding flour and water to the container for each feed, you will end up with a large volume of levain at different stages of fermentation. The yeast and bacteria cells will be fighting over the small amount of food you introduce. If you keep mixing your levain in smaller portions, the yeast and bacteria cells will have a larger food source to live off.

DAY 4

DAY 5–6

Further Notes on Sourdough Levain

Maintaining your levain

Once your levain is ripe (or even if it's not quite ripe yet), you no longer need to bulk it up. To maintain the levain, discard (or use) over half of the levain and then 'feed' it with new flour and water.

To maintain your levain

100 g (3.5 oz) of your preferred flour
100 g (3.5 oz) water
20 g (0.7 oz) levain

1. Weigh the flour and water and combine them in the container with the levain. Stir vigorously until you have a smooth, thick batter.
2. If you're using the levain within the next few days, leave it out at room temperature and continue discarding half and 'feeding' it daily.
3. If it will be longer before you use the levain, cover it tightly and place it in the refrigerator. Remember to take it out and feed it at least once a week – I also usually let the levain sit out overnight to give the yeast time to recuperate before putting it back in the refrigerator.

Using the discarded sourdough levain

Discarding the old levain can seem wasteful. I know, I know. In fact, when I teach sourdough-making workshops, one of the most frequently asked questions is, 'What can I bake with the sourdough discard?'

There is a wide choice of options for using the discarded levain. You can add it to a compost heap. Or feed it to hens. Or perhaps bake with it – try our *Sourdough Waffles* (see page 133) and our *Sourdough and Olive Oil Crackers* (see page 167), which are both recipes we fall back on at home. Other suggestions include creating a sourdough levain pack for a friend and using it to thicken soups, sauces and stews in a similar way to a roux. The internet is inundated with sourdough discard recipes.

Taking a long break from your levain

If you're taking a break from baking, but want to keep your levain active, you can do two things:

Make a thick levain
Feed your levain double the amount of flour to make a thicker, dough-like paste. This thicker batter will maintain the yeast better over long periods of inactivity in the refrigerator.

Dry the levain
Smear the levain on a silicone baking mat and leave it to dry out. Once completely dry, break it into flakes and store it in an airtight container. Dried levain can be stored in this manner for months. To restart it, dissolve 30 g (1 oz) flakes in 100 g (3.5 oz) water and stir in 100 g (3.5 oz) good-quality flour. Keep somewhere warm and continue feeding the levain until you see activity again.

Storing your sourdough levain in the refrigerator

Since getting into baking, it has become more and more apparent that there is a relationship between the health of my sourdough levain and the quality of my baked goods. In an ideal world, my sourdough levain would normally be fed frequently and kept at a steady room temperature, rising and falling and feeding every eight hours. However, that's not practical and would be wasteful if it were not baked with regularly. Slowing down a sourdough levain by storing it in the refrigerator buys you some time and saves flour between feeds. The colder temperatures wreak havoc on the reproduction rate and cause the bacteria and yeast to become dormant. Refrigeration is a common method for storing sourdough levains over extended periods. It allows the levain to remain somewhat viable, while also slowing down the fermentation, so you don't need to feed as frequently. This is important because with every feed comes a discard if you're not baking with it. Without discarding, your sourdough becomes too acidic and will grow exponentially.

Sticking your sourdough levain in the refrigerator will have some ill effects, however. Over time, the acidity of the levain can increase, as the *Lactobacillus* bacteria that give the bread its signature tang continue to produce lactic acid. Acetic acids also build up, even at these lower temperatures. This can cause the sourdough levain to become more and more acidic over time, which affects the yeast cells and the overall balance of your bubbly bread batter.This happens if a sourdough levain is not refreshed or fed regularly while in the refrigerator. The yeast and bacteria enter a hibernative, spore-like state, which can lead to longer fermentation times and weaker rises when you get back to using the levain to make bread. To avoid this, I recommend refreshing or feeding the sourdough levain regularly, even while it's in the refrigerator.

However, the exact feeding ratio that works best for your particular sourdough levain may depend on a variety of factors, including the hydration level of the levain, the type of flour you're using and the specific strains of wild yeast and bacteria in your levain culture. It is important to observe your levain and adjust your feeding ratio as needed based on its behaviour and how it emerges from hibernation. For example, if your levain is still sluggish or not rising well after feeding, you may need to increase the feeding ratio or adjust the temperature of your environment to help it wake up and become more active. That usually means one, two or three consecutive feeds when you want to get back to baking. If the sourdough levain has been in the refrigerator for just a few days, I generally do one feed. Longer than a week, and I discard and feed twice before baking, with a 12-hour gap between feeds. Any longer in the refrigerator and I like to fully wake up the microbes with a third feed before using it in a mix. Usually, it is full of life and doubles in size after eight hours at room temperature, and that's when I know it'll make some beautifully bubbly bread.

Let's troubleshoot

If you see no bubbles or signs of yeast activity after several days of regular feeds, try the following:

× Boost the activity with a friend's healthy levain.
× Make sure your levain is being kept somewhere warm.
× Stir vigorously when you mix in the fresh flour and water to catch any yeast cells on the edges of the jar or container you are using.
× If if it's very warm in your kitchen, be sure that your levain is not too hot. Your yeast is happiest at 25–30°C (77–86°F).
× If a thin layer of liquid collects on the top of your levain, this is often due to problems with the water to flour ratio. You can pour this layer off the top and feed as normal. If this happens, weigh the ingredients to make sure you are adding the right amount of flour and water by volume.

Notes on Sourdough Baking

Baker's percentage

You will notice that our sourdough recipes are divided into three columns: weight, ingredient and baker's percentage. The baker's percentage is a system whereby the weight of every ingredient is calculated as a percentage of the weight of the flour, which is always set at 100 per cent. This approach keeps recipes adaptable and helps bakers maintain the proper balance of ingredients, no matter what the batch size.

The flour is the base of the recipe. If a recipe includes multiple types of flour, like our *Spelt and Toasted Sunflower Seed Sourdough* (see page 110), their combined weight equals 100 per cent.

Invest in a set of digital scales and weigh everything in grams, as precision is key when working with baker's percentages. Practise and experiment by halving or doubling a recipe using the percentage system to build your confidence as a baker. Play around with water percentages and hydration to understand the influence this has on dough handling and final texture. By mastering baker's percentages, you'll gain the flexibility to adapt recipes like a pro and unlock endless creativity in your baking journey. It's the secret to professional results every time.

You will notice, too, that the baker's percentages are measured in grams and kilograms only to allow for accuracy.

How to calculate baker's percentages:

- × Weigh all your ingredients.
- × Divide the weight of each ingredient by the weight of the flour.
- × Multiply the result by 100 to convert to a percentage.

Why do a levain build?

We also use a levain build for a lot of our sourdough recipes. A levain build is a feed between a mature levain and the final dough, allowing us to boost fermentation, flavour and strength. By creating a fresh levain before mixing, we ensure that the yeast and bacteria are at their peak activity, leading to a better rise and more consistency. This step also lets us adjust hydration, flour type, acidity and fermentation time to suit each bread recipe, giving us more precision and consistency in baking but also to better suit the final flavour profile of the baked bread.

Adding inclusions

Including seeds, nuts, dried fruits or herbs is an excellent way to elevate flavour, texture and versatility.

- × Aim for 15–25 per cent of the flour weight in inclusions.
- × Toast seeds and nuts lightly in a dry frying pan for added flavour.
- × Go another step by soaking your seeds in water for 1–2 hours to soften (known as a soaker).
- × Soak dried fruits in tea before straining and patting dry.
- × Blitz herbs with olive oil to create a fragrant paste.
- × Vegetables, such as potatoes, cherry tomatoes and onions can be roasted in advance with good olive oil.
- × Adjust hydration if necessary. Some inclusions, such as soaked seeds or fruits, will add moisture to the dough,while others, like nuts, may require a slight increase in hydration to maintain balance.

Master Recipe:
Country Sourdough

Makes 2 loaves
Time 3 days

Wheat Levain Build

100 g	(3.5 oz) warm water
50 g	(1.8 oz) mature wheat levain
75 g	(2.7 oz) strong white bread flour
25 g	(0.9 oz) wholegrain flour

639 g	warm water	70%
229 g	levain (see above)	25%
685 g	strong white bread flour, plus extra for dusting	75%
229 g	wholegrain flour of your choice	25%
20 g	fine sea salt	2.2%

Baker's note

The wholegrain flour can be made up of a blend of flours or a single type. This is where you have an opportunity to experiment and play. I like equal parts wholegrain rye flour (114 g/4 oz) and wholegrain spelt flour (115 g/4.1oz).

There's something timeless about sourdough bread – a loaf rooted in simplicity, yet brimming with character. It's 100 per cent naturally leavened, showcasing a tangy flavour, a chewy crumb and a dark-baked, blistered crust that crunches with every bite.

Crafted with a blend of wheat, rye and Irish wholegrain spelt flours, this country sourdough balances lightness with depth of flavour. It's the closest we come to a classic white bread, yet it embodies the complexity and soul that define true sourdough.

Perfect for sandwiches, toasting or an open-faced masterpiece, this sourdough is versatile and endlessly satisfying, whether enjoyed simply with butter or as the base for a hearty and healthy meal at breakfast, lunch or dinner. From years of experience teaching sourdough workshops for beginners, I've found that one loaf is never enough when baking at home. You'll have the loaf devoured, warm from the oven with butter, wondering why you didn't make a second. I bake one loaf in a casserole dish (Dutch oven) and one in a loaf tin (pan).

Baking sourdough at home is very rewarding, albeit a time-consuming process. Here's a general timeline guide for making our country sourdough from scratch:

Day one (morning)
Mix flour, water and old levain to create a fresh levain build for baking. Allow to ferment at room temperature for 8–10 hours.

Day one (evening)
Mix flour, water and bubbly levain from the previous step to create a really active levain. Allow to ferment at room temperature overnight for no more than 12 hours.

Day two (morning)
Follow our country sourdough recipe. Perform your stretch and folds. Allow the dough to rise at room temperature for 4 hours, folding every 40 minutes.

Day two (afternoon)
Shape the dough. Place in the banneton and loaf tin (pan). Prove in the refrigerator for a slow, overnight rise.

Day three (flexible)
Preheat the oven, then bake until the bread has a deep, golden-brown crust and a hollow sound when tapped on the bottom.

RECIPE CONTINUED OVERLEAF

Day one

Mix the levain

1 Mix the levain 8 hours before you intend to make the dough. Combine all the ingredients for the wheat levain build in a bowl, cover and leave somewhere warm to ferment. Once the levain passes the float test (see page 97), you are ready to mix your dough.

Day two

2 Pour the water into a large mixing bowl – it should be at a temperature of 26–27°C (79–81°F).
3 Add the levain and allow to dissolve in the water. Ensure you reserve the leftover levain, as this is your levain for the next build and future loaves.
4 Add the bread flour and your chosen wholegrain flour to the mixing bowl. Massage the flour into the water with one hand until there are no visible clumps or pieces of flour left. The dough will resemble an untidy mass at this stage. Clean down the sides of the bowl and also your hand.
5 Cover the bowl with a damp dish towel and leave the dough to rest somewhere warm for 40 minutes. This is the autolyse stage of fermentation.
6 After 40 minutes, the dough should be transformed. It will have turned from an untidy mass into a cohesive dough. The water should have been absorbed and the dough will be stretchy. Now it's time to add the salt. Dissolve the salt in 40 g (1.4 oz) lukewarm water. Incorporate the salt solution into the dough by massaging and breaking the dough apart – it helps to dampen your hand for this step.
7 At first, the dough will tear and rip. Don't panic, as these are the protein strands and bonds breaking apart. Stretch the dough over itself using the sides of the bowl. It will reform into a smooth, uniform dough.
8 Use your hand to clean down the sides of the bowl again and cover with a dish towel. Now the bulk fermentation stage begins. This is your dough's first rise – it will ferment slowly for 4 hours.
9 It's important to consider where you leave the dough to ferment. You want the temperature to be consistent, as the dough will be sensitive to fluctuations. Keep the bowl covered during this time, so the surface isn't in direct contact with the air.

DAY TWO (STEP 9)

A SINGLE FOLD (REPEAT ON EACH 'CORNER')

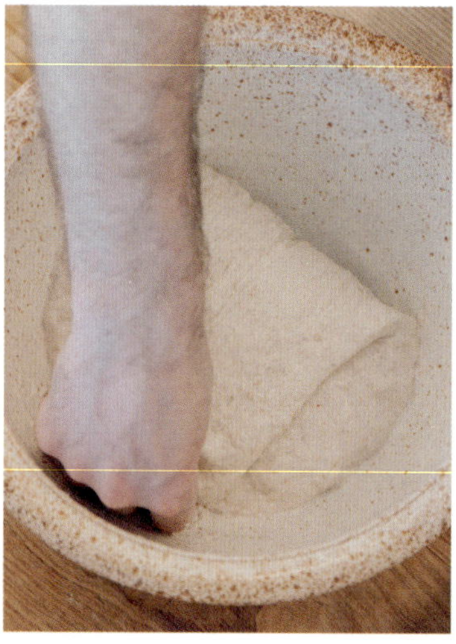

10 Every 30 minutes over the next 4 hours, you will perform folds on the dough. To do this, imagine the bowl has four 'corners'. Dampen your hand with warm water (again, this helps keep the temperature of the dough consistent). Cold water will drop the temperature and prolong the bulk fermentation. Stretch the dough from the bottom of the bowl into the centre. Repeat this at all four 'corners'. Tuck your hand under the dough, releasing it from the sides and bottom of the bowl. Smooth the surface by gently pulling the dough against the edge of the bowl, creating tension. Cover and leave to relax. Be gentle during the folds. The purpose of this stage is to develop flavour and complexity in the bread. The long, slow fermentation also allows tiny gas bubbles to grow and be captured within the gluten structure. During the first two hours, the dough will feel heavier to the touch, turning pillowy and light during the third hour. Be flexible with these timings. Follow your intuition and extend the bulk fermentation time if you notice the dough's activity isn't where it should be.

11 When the dough is pillow-like, it is ready to be divided. Remember, this recipe makes two loaves of bread. Turn out the dough onto a clean work surface, using a damp hand and a dough scraper, and being careful not to deflate it. Divide the dough into two pieces, each weighing 890–900 g (around 1 lb 12 oz–2 lb).

12 Now it's time to preshape each piece of dough into a tight ball. Preshaping a loaf of sourdough is a crucial step in developing structure and creating an even crumb, while maintaining the trapped tiny air bubbles that you worked on developing during the bulk fermentation. To do this, use the dough scraper in one hand (as an extension of your arm), your work surface and your other hand cupped around the dough. Rotate the dough in small circles, tucking the edges under and tightening the surface tension. The dough should become smooth and taut and hold its shape. Repeat for the second loaf.

13 Let the preshaped dough rest, uncovered, on the work surface for 20–25 minutes. During this time, the gluten will relax, making the final shaping easier. Keep an eye on the dough – it will spread slightly but maintain its overall shape. If it flattens excessively, it might need to be preshaped again with more surface tension.

14 While the loaves are resting, grease a 23 x 13 cm (9 x 5 in) loaf tin (pan) with melted butter or sunflower oil and dust the inside of a 1 kg (2 lb 4 oz) capacity banneton with flour, including the bottom and sides.

DAY TWO (STEP 11)

PRESHAPING THE LOAVES

15 Once the loaves have rested, it's time for the main shaping. First, let's shape the loaf that you will bake in the loaf tin. Lightly flour the work surface. Using the dough scraper, release the dough from the work surface. Be swift and confident in your movement. Turn the preshaped dough over onto the work surface, so what was the bottom is now facing upward. Stretch the bottom edge up into the centre of the round. Then stretch the sides inwards, gently pulling the left side over two thirds of the round, followed by the right side, overlapping the dough below. Finally, imagine the top part of the dough has a left and right ear, and gently stretch those ears/corners up and over the folds you created. Roll the dough over itself, so the seam is now on the work surface.

16 Using the dough scraper and the other hand cupped, push the dough into an oblong, batard shape (a short French oval or oblong bâtard). Pick the shaped loaf up with your hand and dough scraper and place, seam side down, in the prepared loaf tin. Gently settle the dough into the corners. Cover the surface with a dish towel and leave to relax for 15–20 minutes.

17 Now let's shape the loaf that will prove in the banneton. Using the guidelines outlined in step 14, shape the loaf using the same sequence of folds to create tension and delicately trap the gas. With the seam on the work surface, use the dough scraper to release the dough in one swift movement. Flip the dough into your palms, gently cradling the weight. Transfer to the floured banneton, smooth side down and seam side up. Pinch the seam closed. Cover with a dish towel and leave to rest with the first loaf.

18 Clear a shelf in the refrigerator and transfer both loaves to the shelf to slow down the fermentation process overnight. This step will develop the complex tang of the sourdough. You can leave the loaves in the refrigerator for 18–36 hours.

DAY TWO (STEP 14)

SHAPING A LOAF INTO A BANNETON

Day three

Bake the loaves

1 Preheat the oven to as hot as it can go, preferably 240°C (500°F) or above. Place a casserole dish (Dutch oven) in the oven while the oven is preheating.

2 Take both loaves from the refrigerator. Turn the dough out of the banneton onto a small piece of baking parchment (seam side down and smooth side up). Brush off any excess flour. Using a sharp knife or a bread lame, score the surface of the dough. Hold the blade at a slight angle for a deeper cut. Repeat the score on the dough in the loaf tin – a single-line score works well to allow the loaf to expand evenly during the bake.

3 The next step takes some organising. Gather some oven gloves (mitts) and dish towels. Take the preheated casserole dish (Dutch oven) out of the oven and remove the lid. Carefully lift the banneton dough, using the baking parchment, and gently lower it into the casserole dish. Clamp on the lid and place on the middle shelf of the oven. Place the loaf tin on the same shelf beside it. Bake both loaves for 25 minutes, then remove the casserole lid, turn the oven temperature down to 200°C (425°F) and bake the loaf tin loaf for a further 20 minutes and the casserole loaf for a further 25 minutes.

4 Once baked, the loaves should have a lightness to them. Remove from the oven and leave to cool for a couple of hours before slicing into them but it can be hard to resist tearing off a chunk.

DAY THREE (STEPS 2–3)

SCORING AND BAKING THE LOAF

Spelt and Toasted Sunflower Seed Sourdough

Makes 2 loaves
Time 3 days

Wheat Levain Build

50 g	(1.8 oz) mature wheat levain
100 g	(3.5 oz) water
75 g	(2.7 oz) strong white bread flour
25 g	(0.9 oz) wholemeal spelt flour

624 g	warm water	74%
212 g	levain (see above)	25%
422 g	wholegrain spelt flour	50%
338 g	white spelt flour	40%
20 g	malted flour	10%
20 g	fine sea salt	2.3%

Inclusions

260 g	(9.5 oz) sunflower seeds

We work alongside a wonderful, Irish grain-growing and milling company in the Midlands – The Little Mill (see page 115). They produce high-quality, freshly milled flour a 30-minute drive from Shane's family home. Spelt flour has become more readily available over the last few years. You can source it from your local health food shop. Spelt flour can be a little sticky to work with – this loaf is also high in hydration, pushing over 70 per cent. We like to bake it in a loaf tin (pan) for ease of shaping and slicing once cooled.

This loaf blends wholemeal spelt and white spelt, resulting in a caramel-colour crumb with subtle nutty flavours from the grain. The blend works perfectly with the toasted aroma and flavours of the sunflower seeds. The crumb is soft and spongey and reminds me of toasted crumpets, and is most delicious toasted, for soaking up melted butter.

Day one

1 Mix the levain 8 hours before you intend to mix the dough. Combine all the ingredients for the wheat levain build in a bowl, cover and leave somewhere warm to ferment. When the levain passes the float test (see page 97), you are ready to mix the dough.

Day two

1 Pour the water into a large mixing bowl – the temperature should be 37°C (100°F). Add the levain to the water to dissolve and disperse. Next, add all the flours. Use your hand to massage the flour thoroughly into the water until there are no dry pieces of flour left. The dough should have an uneven texture. Cover with a damp dish towel and leave to rest for 30 minutes.

2 Preheat the oven to 180°C (390°F).

3 While the dough is resting, toast 110 g (3.9 oz) of the sunflower seeds on a baking tray (pan) in the oven for 8 minutes. Once lightly toasted, add a splash of water (about 15 g/0.5 oz) and leave to cool.

4 After 30 minutes, add the salt to the dough. Dampen your hand first before squeezing and massaging the dough between your fingers. The dough will break apart initially, but then reform into a cohesive mass as you turn it over itself in the bowl. Fold the dough over itself a couple of times. Rest for a further 30 minutes.

5 Add the toasted sunflower seeds to the dough and fold this over itself with a damp hand until it is smooth again. You will now fold the dough four times over a three-hour period, every 45 minutes. This is the bulk fermentation stage, when the dough rises. Don't rush or hurry this step. During the folds, keep the dough in a warm place. To fold the dough, use a hand dampened with warm water (cold water will reduce the dough temperature and slow down the bulk fermentation stage) to pull and stretch the dough from the bottom up over itself. Stretch even sections of the dough. Avoid being forceful with this motion, as you don't want the gluten development to tear

or rip and you don't want to deflate the dough. You are aiming to trap the lovely gas bubbles as it bulk ferments.

6 After 3 hours, turn out the dough onto a clean, dry work surface. Round the dough and divide in half. Remember, you're making two loaves – each one should weigh 880 g (around 2 lb).
7 Round the two pieces of dough into tight balls by using the dough scraper and a cupped hand – the surface should be tight, smooth and holding tension. If the dough is ripping, this is a sign to stop rounding. Cover with a dish towel to prevent the dough forming a skin and leave to rest for 20 minutes. Grease two 23 x 13 cm (9 x 5 in) loaf tins (pans) with melted butter or sunflower oil and put the remaining sunflower seeds into a medium bowl.
8 For the final shaping of the loaves, slide the dough scraper under one of the loaves in a swift, confident movement. Round the loaf using the edge of the dough scraper and your other hand until it is smooth and tight. Push the dough into an oval shape using the tension of the dough on the work surface, the dough scraper and your other hand. Flip the dough over, so the tight, smooth side is in the palm of one hand, then pinch together and flip back into the greased loaf tin. Repeat for the second loaf.
9 Scatter 75 g (2.7 oz) of the sunflower seeds over each loaf. Leave the dough to relax in the tins for 30 minutes. Cover with a dish towel and transfer to the refrigerator until the next day.

Day three

1 When you are ready to bake the loaves, preheat the oven to 240°C (500°F). Score the loaves with two deep lines, splash the surface with water and place on the middle shelf of the oven. Splash the floor of the oven with half a cup of water, too.
2 Close the oven door and reduce the temperature to 220°C (475°C). Bake for 25 minutes, then turn the oven down to 200°C (425°F) and bake for a further 20 minutes.
3 At the halfway point, rotate the loaves if you know your oven has hot spots. Check that the internal temperature of the loaves is 98°C (208°F), then remove from the oven immediately and allow to cool completely before slicing.

THE LITTLE MILL We would argue that flour is the most important ingredient you need as a baker. Returning to Ireland from San Francisco, where we worked in bakeries that connect directly to the grower and miller, we knew we wanted to do the same at home. First, we found Kells Wholemeal, the sister company to The Little Mill which imports good-quality Canadian, French, Polish and UK flours. Both were set up by the Mosse Family in 1982. Seven generations of miller knowledge. The mill is just north of Ballyragget, in County Laois – about 30 minutes from where Shane grew up and where all his close and large extended family still live.

Located in the picturesque village of Bennettsbridge, County Kilkenny, The Little Mill is one of the only mills in the country still producing stoneground wholemeal (wholegrain) and sifted flours on a large scale for the bakery trade in Ireland. It is nestled on the banks of the River Nore, with the mill dating back to 1840. Today, nearly all the grain comes from one of three farms, no more than 20 km (12 miles) from the mill. In recent years, Bill and Robert Mosse have begun to offer native Irish species of wheat and grain, including Ølands and purple wheat.

WAKELY
L031-S001

Cissy's Rye

Makes 1 loaf
Time 2 days

Rye Levain Build

50 g	(1.8 oz) rye levain
250 g	(8.8 oz) water
250 g	(8.8 oz) light rye flour, plus 1 tablespoon for dusting

---

125 g	water	76%
500 g	rye levain	303%
18 g	black treacle (molasses)	12%
150 g	wholegrain rye flour	100%
8 g	fine sea salt	4.8%
100 g	blend of pumpkin seeds, flax/linseeds, black sesame seeds, white sesame seeds and poppy seeds	

Baker's note

Serve with boiled eggs as a delicious baker's breakfast.

Rye flour has a unique and robust sour flavour, even before it is fermented. It imparts a rich and complex profile to bread and is an amazing injection of flavour. This recipe was developed by pastry chef Cissy Difford after a week-long trip to Copenhagen and is styled off a Danish loaf made with treacle (molasses) for those deep caramel aromas that work so well with rye flour. This loaf is best baked and left to cure for a day. The delicate interior crumb will have time to set and won't be too tacky when you go to slice it for toast or sandwiches. The shelf life of this sourdough is excellent, and we often get five days out of one loaf.

Day one

1 Prepare the rye levain. This is more stable than wheat flour levain, so you have a longer window to work with it. Note that the temperature of the water will influence how quickly the levain will ferment. During the colder months, you should use lukewarm water, but cold tap water in the summer. Combine the old levain, water and flour in a container or bowl. Mix until you have a smooth paste, then cover with a lid or dish towel.

2 Leave the levain for 12 hours and a maximum of 24 hours. Keep an eye on the levain as it ferments. If the temperature in your kitchen is warmer than normal, use the levain closer to 12 hours than 24.

Day two

1 Once the levain is ready, you can mix the dough. Put the water, rye levain and treacle into a large bowl. Mix until the treacle is evenly distributed and dissolved. Next, add the flour, salt and 85 g (3 oz) of seed blend. Using a rubber spatula or wooden spoon, bring all the ingredients together into a smooth, even dough. Cover with a damp dish towel and leave to rest for 30 minutes.

2 While the dough is resting, grease a 23 x 13 cm (9 x 5 in) loaf tin (pan) with melted butter or sunflower oil. After 30 minutes, scrape the dough into the tin, wet your hand with cold water and smooth the surface of the dough. Gently tap the tin on the work surface, so the dough settles into the edges and corners.

3 Dust the top of the loaf with a tablespoon of light rye flour and the remaining seed mix. Leave somewhere warm to prove for 1½–2 hours. The surface of the loaf will crack. Once the loaf has doubled in size and the surface has cracked, it is ready to bake.

4 Preheat the oven to 230°C (475°F). Bake the loaf for 30 minutes, then reduce the temperature to 200°C (425°F) and bake for a further 30 minutes. If your oven has hot spots, rotate the loaf halfway through.

5 Check the internal temperature of the loaf with a digital thermometer – it should be 98°C (208°F). If the temperature isn't there yet, return the loaf to the oven for a further 10 minutes and check again.

6 Remove from the oven and cool in the tin on a wire rack. Once set and cool, you can remove from the tin. If stored correctly, this loaf can remain fresh for a week.

Sourdough Focaccia

Makes 1 focaccia
Time 2 days

Wheat Levain Build

100 g	(3.5 oz) strong white bread flour
100 g	(3.5 oz) lukewarm water
50 g	(1.75 oz) mature wheat levain

320 g	water	69.5%
115 g	ripe levain	25%
345 g	strong white bread flour	75%
115 g	finely milled wholemeal (whole-wheat) flour	25%
10 g	fine sea salt	2.2%
25 g	extra virgin olive oil	5.5%

Flaky sea salt
Extra virgin olive oil

This is a soft, pillowy sourdough focaccia based on the *Country Sourdough* recipe (see page 105). While the focaccia is proving, you can think about adding different flavourings. Thinly slice potatoes and sprinkle them over the stippled dough along with olive oil and thyme. Or roast some sliced shallots with balsamic vinegar to add to your dough. We also love to top the focaccia we sell at the bakery with cherry tomatoes locally grown by the Happy Pear Farm.

Day one

1. Mix the levain 8 hours before you intend to mix the dough. Combine all the ingredients for the wheat levain build in a bowl, cover and leave somewhere warm to ferment. When the levain passes the float test (see page 97), you are ready to mix the dough.
2. Pour the water into a large mixing bowl – it should be at a temperature of 28–29°C (82–84°F). Add the levain, stirring with one hand to dissolve.
3. Add the bread flour and wholemeal flour to the bowl. If you can't source finely milled wholemeal flour, sift coarse wholemeal to achieve the same consistency. Massage the flour into the water with one hand until there are no visible clumps of flour left. The dough will resemble an uneven mass at this stage. Clean down the sides of the bowl and also your hand. Cover the bowl with a dish towel and leave somewhere warm for 30 minutes.
4. After 30 minutes, the dough should have transformed from an uneven mass into a cohesive dough. The water should have been absorbed and the dough will be stretchy.
5. Now scatter the salt over the surface of the dough. To incorporate the salt into the dough, use a damp hand to massage and break the dough apart. At first, the dough will tear and rip. Don't panic, as this is the protein strands and bonds breaking apart. Stretch the dough over itself using the sides of the bowl. It will reform into a smooth, uniform dough. Clean down the sides of the bowl again and also your hand. Cover with a dish towel and leave to rest for 20 minutes. Again, leave the bowl somewhere warm.
6. In a small dish or ramekin, combine the oil with 50 g (1.8 oz) lukewarm water. Remember, it's crucial that the temperature of the dough doesn't drop. You are aiming to maintain a temperature of 28–29°C (82–84°F).
7. Add the olive oil and water mix to the dough. This will look like a lot of liquid to mix into the already highly hydrated dough. Don't worry, as it will be absorbed. Gently massage the oil into the dough. As when you added the salt, the dough with tear and rip. Be gentle here, as the dough will come back together. Massage a couple of times before switching to a folding motion to bring the dough back to a smooth, even mass. Cover with a dish towel and leave for 30 minutes. Now the bulk fermentation begins.
8. Every 30 minutes, for a total of 3 hours, you will fold the dough. See step 9 of the *Country Sourdough* recipe (see page 107).

9 Line a 28 x 36 cm (11 x 14 in) baking tray (pan) with baking parchment – this really helps prevent the focaccia from sticking during the baking and breaking your heart. Drizzle generously with olive oil.
10 At the 3-hour point, dampen your hand with warm water and release the dough from the sides of the mixing bowl, then tip it into the tray. Gently tease the corners of the dough into the tray but try not to rip the dough. Cover with a dish towel to avoid a skin forming and leave to relax for 20 minutes. After this time, the dough should have spread out to roughly fill the dimensions of the tray. Keeping the tray covered, place it in the refrigerator. I recommend clearing a shelf ahead of time for this.

Day two

1 Make a mental note of when you would like to enjoy your focaccia. It takes a further 2 hours 30 minutes to prove at room temperature. Set an alarm and pull the tray from the refrigerator. I like to place the tray in the oven to provide a humid environment to prove my focaccia.
2 After 1 hour 30 minutes of proving, it's time to stipple the dough to create those delicious, oil-filled pockets. Drizzle the surface of the dough with more olive oil, about 25 g (0.9 oz). With damp fingers, push halfway down into the dough, while also trying to push out to the corners of the tray. Repeat this over the surface of the focaccia and then return it to the cold oven for a further 1 hour.
3 When you are ready to bake, remove the focaccia from the oven before preheating it to 220°C (475°F). Bake the focaccia in the oven for 15 minutes, then reduce the temperature to 200°C (425°F) and bake for a further 15 minutes. The halfway point is a perfect time to rotate the tray if you know your oven has hot spots.
4 Remove the focaccia from the oven and leave to cool for a few minutes on a wire rack. Once the focaccia has firmed up and isn't too delicate, remove from the tray to cool.

Pan de Cristal

Makes 3–4 small rolls
Time 4 hours 30 minutes

225 g	strong white bread flour, plus extra for dusting	90%
25 g	whole spelt flour	10%
50 g	old levain	20%
250 g	water	100%
1 g	osmotolerant yeast	0.3%
6 g	fine sea salt	2.3%
Olive oil, for greasing		

Pan de cristal or 'glass bread' is one of those crunchy, rustic regional favourites. Originating from the Catalonia region of Spain, where its called *pa de vidre*, the dough relies heavily on high hydration, accurate scaling and plenty of patience. Be patient. It will come together. This crusty, ciabatta-style bread makes the ultimate sandwich bread but also works well for *pan con tomate* (Spanish tomato bread) or grilled garlicky toast.

1. Massage all the ingredients together by hand in a medium mixing bowl until they form an uneven mass. The mixture will be very sticky, so dampen your hand with warm water first. Cover with a dish towel and leave for 20 minutes. The dough will be very wet and loose.
2. While the dough is resting, lightly grease a 20 x 12 x 12 cm (8 x 4¾ x 4¾ in) container with oil. A container of this size will allow the dough to rise and grow, while at the same time giving it support and structure.
3. Transfer the dough to the container and perform a coil fold. To do this, with warm, wet hands, reach under the dough and stretch the middle upward until it releases from the bottom and sides of the container. Roll the dough forward, away from you, allowing it to fold over itself. Continue doing this until the dough is shaped like a log. Rotate the dough 90 degrees and leave to rest for 20 minutes. Repeat four more coil folds, resting between each fold. (Be light-handed as you handle the dough. As you repeat the coil folds, the dough will develop more structure and become easier to handle.)
4. After five coil folds, cover the container with a dish towel and leave to prove for 50–60 minutes. Line a baking tray (pan) with baking parchment.
5. Heavily flour the surface of the dough and the work surface. Release the dough from the sides of the container. To do this, use a swift and confident motion, cutting down along the edge of the container with a dough scraper. The flour from the surface of the dough will act as a barrier, preventing the dough from sticking to the edges while you work your way around all four sides. Quickly invert the container onto the floured work surface. Allow the dough to fall out. Don't pull or stretch the dough.
6. Cut the dough into three equal pieces. Be quick with your cuts, being careful not to deflate the dough. Transfer the pieces to the lined baking tray, using the dough knife and your hand to lift them carefully from the work surface.
7. Once the pieces of dough are on the baking tray, use a pastry brush to dust off the excess flour. Cover the tray lightly with a dish towel and leave for 1 hour to rise.
8. While the dough is rising, preheat the oven to 240°C (500°F) – the oven should be rigorously hot.
9. Place the loaves in the oven and bake for 17–20 minutes until they have deeply caramelised crusts. Remove from the oven and leave to cool on a wire rack before eating (see our suggestions on how to use your *pan de cristal* to make a special Scéal sandwich on page 130).

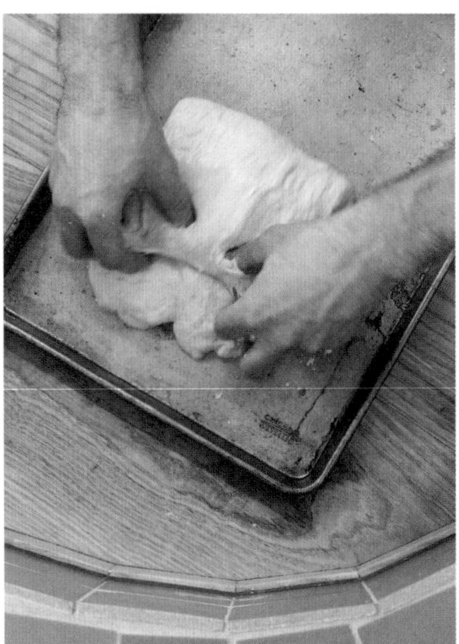

Scéal Sandwiches

Mortadella, Peach, Buffalo Mozzarella and Mojo Verde

Generously spread *Mojo Verde* (see page 198) on both sides of the bread. Gently ripple and undulate waves of mortadella over the bread, top with torn pieces of mozzarella and thinly sliced peach. Drizzle with olive oil before closing the two halves of the sandwich together.

Grilled Halloumi and New-season Tomato with Bread and Butter Pickles

Grill thick slices of halloumi cheese in a frying pan. Thinly slice tomatoes and season to taste with salt and pepper. First, drizzle the bread with olive oil, then top with tomato slices and a generous mound of *Bread and Butter Pickles* (see page 199). Add the grilled halloumi and finish with a handful of dressed salad leaves – something peppery like mustard leaf or mizuna works a treat. You can replace the pickles with thinly sliced raw courgette (zucchini) or shop-bought gherkins (dill pickles).

Jambon-beurre

This is a perfect sandwich to make after Christmas, as you will probably have the most delicious ham left over. Liberally spread salted butter on both pieces of bread. Next, add a thick layer of wholegrain mustard – choose one that has a little natural sweetness. Lay thin slices of the best-quality ham on top. It's even better if you prepare the ham yourself. Thinly slice 8–10 cornichons (small dill pickles), scatter them over the ham and finish with a crack of black pepper.

Beetroot Jam, Walnut Miso Crunch, Goat's Cheese and Radicchio

The *Walnut Miso Crunch* recipe (see page 199) was developed by our really great pal Katie Sanderson – who is co-owner of the brilliant White Mausu. They no longer sell this by the jar, but when they did, let me tell you, it was INSANELY addictive. Katie would make separate big momma jars of the stuff for me, which I'd consume by the spoonful – eating half a jar in one sitting and having a tingly tongue and mouth afterwards from all the umami goodness. It is brilliant in a cheese toastie or on a cheese board. Add it to your larder list immediately.

To make the sandwich, spread the bread with *Beetroot Jam* (see page 198), and liberal spoonfuls of walnut miso crunch on top. Keep some of the oil aside from the crunch and use it to dress some bitter radicchio leaves. Lay the leaves over the beetroot jam and walnut miso crunch. Crumble over salty, soft goat's cheese such as St Tola or Killeen.

Sourdough Waffles with Maple Whipped Butter

Makes 4 waffles
Time 1 hour

55 g	(1.94 oz) unsalted butter
230 g	(8.1 oz) buttermilk
50 g	(1.8 oz) egg (about 1 UK medium/US large egg)
50 g	(1.8 oz) leftover levain
125 g	(4.4 oz) plain (all-purpose) flour
7 g	(1½ teaspoons) caster (superfine) sugar
2 g	(½ teaspoon) fine sea salt
2 g	(½ teaspoon) bicarbonate of soda (baking soda)
20–25g	(0.7–0.9 oz) water (if needed)

For the Maple Whipped Butter

150 g	(5.3 oz) unsalted butter (at room temperature)
2 g	(½ teaspoon) flaky sea salt
75 g	(2.7 oz) maple syrup

This recipe is adapted from an article written by Maurizio Leo for *Food 52*. We make these waffles on a weekly basis in our house. Leftover or spent sourdough levain is always to hand if you are baking sourdough regularly. You can use leftover levain from the *Country Sourdough* (see page 105) or *Spelt and Toasted Sunflower Seed Sourdough* (see page 111). Try not to use a levain that has become very acidic, as the texture of the waffles will be gummy and not as enjoyable. You can also use ripe levain. If you don't have a waffle iron, the batter also works brilliantly for thick, American-style pancakes – just leave out the water for a stiffer batter.

1. To make the waffle batter, melt the butter in a small saucepan over a medium heat, then let it cool. While the butter is cooling, whisk together the buttermilk, egg and leftover levain in a large mixing bowl.
2. Next, add the flour, sugar, salt and bicarbonate of soda. Whisk until you have a smooth batter. Finally, add the melted butter. If the batter is very thick, add 25 g (0.9 oz) cold water. Leave the batter to sit for 10 minutes.
3. While the batter is resting, preheat the waffle iron.
4. To make the maple whipped butter, beat the butter with the salt in a medium mixing bowl until pale and light. It's important that the butter and maple syrup are at the same temperature. If one is cold, the butter will seize and split. Gradually add the maple syrup, beating between each drizzle. Beat until pale and fluffy. This can be done by hand or with a food processor or hand-held electric whisk.
5. To make the waffles, pour one ladle of batter into the waffle iron and cook for 4–5 minutes until golden brown, crisp and light. Repeat with the remaining batter.
6. Enjoy the waffles with a generous dollop of maple butter, crispy smoked bacon and sausages.

Granny's Brown Bread

Makes 1 loaf
Time 2 hours 30 minutes

250 g	(8.8 oz) plain (all-purpose) flour, plus extra for dusting
250 g	(8.8 oz) wholemeal (whole-wheat) flour
6 g	(1½ teaspoons) bicarbonate of soda (baking soda)
6 g	(1½ teaspoons) fine sea salt
380–420 g	(13.4–14.8 oz) buttermilk

My granny, a humble home baker, called her soda breads 'cakes', a fitting name for their indulgent flavour and tender crumb. She baked six cakes daily – three brown and three curnie cakes (traditional Irish brown bread made with dried fruit). Granny nourished her family of 17 children with her signature bread, which was rich in tradition and love.

Granny's brown bread was always served thickly sliced, slathered with butter and crowned with honey. We often had a slice for dessert. Granny's touch lay in her gentle mixing, mindful of incorporating air and working with a light hand to avoid developing gluten. She would score a cross on each loaf before baking 'to let the fairies out' – a tradition passed down through the generations.

Though I've never quite matched Granny's skill, the practice of making her bread keeps her memory alive. This recipe, shared with me by my Uncle Dominic, captures the essence of Granny's craft. It's not just a recipe; it's a ritual – one steeped in tradition, love and a little bit of magic.

1. Preheat the oven to 220°C (475°F).
2. Put the flours, bicarbonate of soda and salt into a large mixing bowl and mix together with your fingertips. Be light and playful, incorporating as much air as possible.
3. Make a well in the centre of the dry ingredients and pour in most of the buttermilk. Hold back 20–40 ml (1.5–3 tablespoons). Mix the dough with your hands until it barely comes together. If the dough seems dry, gradually add the buttermilk you held back until you achieve a soft and slightly sticky consistency. Avoid overmixing. The dough should be falling off your hand.
4. Turn the dough out onto a lightly floured surface and gently bring it together with your hands to form a round loaf. A gentle touch is required for this step. The loaf should be approximately 15 cm (6 in) in diameter and about 5 cm (2 in) tall.
5. Place the loaf on a floured baking tray (pan). Use a sharp knife to make a deep cross on top of the loaf. You can cut one line and two smaller lines perpendicular to this line – this will give a taller and more rounded loaf once baked.
6. Bake in the oven for 35–40 minutes or until the bread is dark golden brown and sounds hollow when tapped on the bottom.
7. Remove the bread from the oven and transfer to a wire rack to cool. Wrap a damp dish towel around the loaf – the steam will soften the crust. Allow to cool completely before slicing.
8. Enjoy the bread sliced thick, slathered in salted butter and drizzled with local honey.

Master Recipe:
Shokupan

Makes 2 loaves or 12–13 buns
Time 2-3 days

For the Yudane

60 g	(2 oz) whole milk
60 g	(2 oz) strong white bread flour

For the Dough

90–100 g	(3.2–3.5 oz) yudane (see above)
100 g	(3.5 oz) egg (2 UK large eggs/US extra-large eggs)
200 g	(7 oz) whole milk
500 g	(1 lb 2 oz) strong white bread flour
40 g	(1.4 oz) caster (superfine) sugar
20 g	(0.75 oz) honey
10 g	(0.5 oz) fine sea salt
7 g	(1½ teaspoons) osmotolerant yeast
50 g	(1.8 oz) unsalted butter (at room temperature)

To Make Loaves

Batch of *Shokupan* dough
Egg Wash (see page 209)
Olive oil, for greasing

To Make Buns

Batch of *Shokupan* dough
Egg Wash (see page 209)

Baker's note

If you are using the shokupan buns as burger buns, brush them with melted butter while they are still hot from the oven for a delicious sheen.

Shokupan – or Japanese milk bread – is incredibly soft, light and fluffy. It is a brilliant everyday loaf and easy to slice for toast or sandwiches. Surprisingly, Japanese milk bread stays fresher and more tender for longer, which is due to a technique called the yudane, whereby a portion of the flour is precooked. Yudane is a roux made with a 1:1 ratio of flour to water. Our recipe uses whole milk for added richness and a deeper colour on the crust once baked.

Gelatinising the starch with boiling milk allows the starch to take on more liquid, keeping the inside of the bread moist. If you can't source osmotolerant yeast, you can replace it with fast-action dried yeast.

This buttery, soft dough is so versatile. You can create countless bakes with it, such as our glazed buns (see page 139), *Matthew's Nduja Buns* (see page 148) and *Coffee and Walnut Twists* (see page 142).

RECIPE CONTINUED OVERLEAF

Day one

1 To make the yudane, bring the milk to the boil in a small saucepan. Transfer to a bowl and mix with the flour until you have an uneven dough. Cover the bowl with a damp dish towel and leave to rest at room temperature for a minimum of 4 hours, preferably overnight.

Day two

1 Put the yudane, egg and milk into a stand mixer fitted with the dough hook attachment. Add the flour, sugar, honey, salt and yeast.

2 Mix at medium speed for 10 minutes. You are aiming to achieve 90 per cent dough development. The dough should clean the sides of the bowl.

3 After 10 minutes, add the softened butter and mix until fully incorporated – a further 5–8 minutes.

4 Cover the bowl with a damp dish towel and leave in a warm place to prove. You want the dough to double in size, which can take about 2 hours, depending on the temperature of your kitchen.

5 Once the dough has doubled in size and is noticeably puffy, knock it back. To do this, press down on the dough with your fist or palm until all the gas has been expelled.

6 Now the dough is ready to shape into a loaf or buns. If you are using the dough to make *Coffee and Walnut Twists* or *Matthew's Nduja Buns* (see pages 143 and 149), press the dough into a large rectangle, cover with cling film (plastic wrap) and chill in the refrigerator for 1 hour, or overnight.

TO MAKE SHOKUPAN BUNS

To make shokupan loaves

1. Grease two 23 x 13 cm (9 x 5 in) loaf tins (pans) and set aside.
2. Scrape the dough onto a clean, un-floured work surface. Using a dough scraper, divide the dough into four equal balls, each weighing 250 g (8.8 oz). Shape each ball into a tight round. To do this, ball the dough on a flat surface and roll it over on itself a few times, rotating each time to keep it round. Finish shaping the dough by pulling it carefully towards you and sealing the bottom tightly to form a smooth, even surface.
3. Place two rounds of dough in each greased loaf pan. Loosely cover the dough with cling film (plastic wrap) to stop a skin forming. A skin will prevent the dough from proving to its full potential. Place the loaves somewhere warm and leave to prove for 1 hour 30 minutes.
4. Preheat the oven to 180°C (390°F).
5. Once the loaves have proved, brush gently with egg wash before placing in the oven. Bake for 30–35 minutes until golden brown. Check the internal temperature of the loaves with a digital thermometer – once fully baked, they should be 90–95°C (194–203°F). If the loaves haven't reached the right internal temperature, bake for a further 5 minutes.
6. Remove the tins from the oven and place on a wire rack to cool. The loaves will be very delicate fresh from the oven, so allow to cool in the tins for 5–10 minutes before removing and leaving to cool completely.

To make shokupan buns

1. Scrape the dough onto a clean, un-floured work surface. Using a dough scraper, divide the dough into 12 or 13 balls, each weighing 75 g (2.7 oz).
2. Shape each ball into a tight round. To do this, ball the dough on a flat surface and roll it over on itself a few times, rotating each time to keep it round. Finish shaping the dough by pulling it carefully towards you and sealing the bottom tightly to form a smooth, even surface.
3. Transfer the dough balls to a baking sheet lined with baking parchment. Cover lightly with cling film and leave to prove for 1 hour 30 minutes until puffy and delicate to the touch.
4. Preheat the oven to 180°C (390°F). Gently brush each bun with egg wash or, alternatively, spray them with water. Bake for 12–15 minutes until deep golden brown.
5. Remove the buns from the oven and place on a wire rack to cool.

(STEPS 1–3)

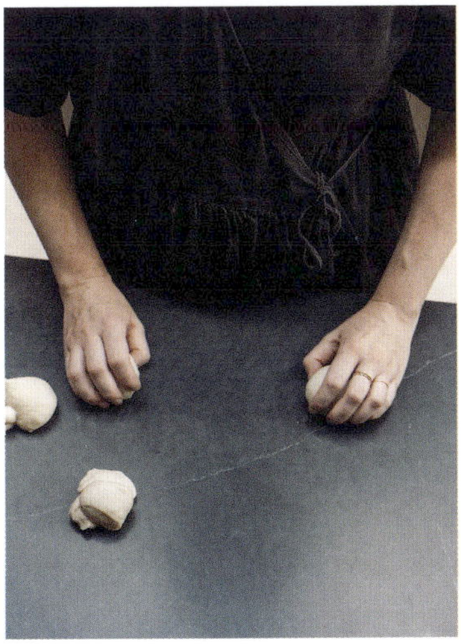

Coffee and Walnut Twists

Makes 10 buns
Time Master recipe + 1 day

Batch of *Shokupan* dough (see page 136)
Egg Wash (see page 209)

For the Walnut and Coffee Filling

90 g (3.2 oz) walnuts
90 g (3.2 oz) Demerara sugar
90 g (3.2 oz) unsalted butter (at room temperature)
2 g (½ teaspoon) flaky sea salt
20 g (0.7 oz) freshly brewed coffee, cooled

For the Espresso Glaze

100 g (3.5 oz) caster (superfine) sugar
100 g (3.5 oz) espresso or freshly brewed coffee

For the Toasted Walnut Brittle

50 g (1.7 oz) walnuts
50 g (1.7 oz) caster (superfine) sugar

The classic flavour pairing – coffee and walnuts. Here, our soft, buttery Japanese milk bread dough is swirled with a sweet paste of toasted walnuts, Demerara sugar and fresh coffee. It is evocative of a Swedish cardamom bun in shape and style. In the bakery, we use leftover espresso from our coffee bar to make the espresso glaze. You can brew your own or use instant powdered coffee. The walnut brittle is addictive – try sprinkling the leftovers over yoghurt or your porridge (oatmeal).

Day one

1 Once proved and knocked back, press the dough into a 20 x 30 cm (8 x 12 in) rectangle, place on a baking tray lined with baking parchment, cover with cling film (plastic wrap) and then transfer to the refrigerator to chill for a minimum 4 of hours and a maximum of 24 hours.

Day two

1 Toast the walnuts for the filling and brittle. Preheat the oven to 180°C (390°F) and toast the walnuts on a baking tray (pan) for 8–10 minutes. Alternatively, you can toast them in a dry frying pan until deep golden brown and fragrant. Leave to cool.

2 To make the walnut and coffee filling, beat together the sugar and butter until smooth, light and airy. Chop the 90 g (3.25 oz) toasted walnuts and add to the creamed sugar and butter along with the salt. Finally, slowly beat in the cold coffee until it is fully incorporated and the mixture is smooth again. Leave at room temperature until you're ready to make the buns.

3 To make the espresso glaze, add the sugar and coffee to a small saucepan. Bring to a boil for 2 minutes. Remove from the heat and set aside to cool.

4 To make the walnut brittle, line a baking tray with baking parchment or a silicone baking mat. Make a dry caramel by melting the sugar in a saucepan over a medium heat. Stir the sugar until a deep amber caramel forms. Remove from the heat and add the 50 g (1.75 oz) toasted walnuts. Coat the nuts in the caramel, working quickly. Tip onto the baking tray. Leave to harden and cool completely.

5 Break the brittle into small pieces and pulse in a food processor until it resembles coarse breadcrumbs. If you don't have a food processor, chop with a knife until you have the right consistency. Remove the dough from the refrigerator, place on a lightly floured surface and roll out to a larger rectangle, 40 cm (16 in) long and 25 cm (10 in) wide. Ensure the long side of the dough is parallel to you.

6 Spread the walnut and coffee filling lengthways over two thirds of the dough, then fold the empty third of the dough into the middle and the remaining third over the top, as you would fold a letter.

7 Return the dough to the baking tray, cover with cling film and put in the refrigerator to chill and rest for 30 minutes.

8 After 30 minutes, remove the dough from the refrigerator and place on a lightly floured surface. Make sure to rotate the dough 90 degrees. The way I remember this is to imagine that the open fold of the letter is facing you.

9 Roll the dough into a rectangle using an even pressure until it is 8 mm (½ in) thick. Using a sharp knife or pizza wheel, cut the dough into 10 strips, 4 cm (1½ in) wide.

10 Working with one piece of dough at a time, lay a strip on a clean, un-floured surface with the long side facing you. Using your palms, gently roll the dough in opposite directions until it begins to spiral.

11 Holding an end in one hand, rotate and spiral the other end to form a snail shape. Tuck the tail end underneath the dough and press down with the palm of your hand. Repeat for each twist.

12 Line two baking trays with baking parchment. Place the twists on the trays, leaving 6 cm (2½ in) between each one to provide space for the dough to prove.

13 Leave the twists somewhere warm to prove for 1–2 hours. Or, alternatively, use the oven as a proving chamber. Once proved, the buns will be pillowy and the layers pushing apart.

14 Preheat the oven to 180°C (390°F). Brush the twists gently with egg wash and bake for 15–18 minutes until golden and soft. Remove the twists from the oven and brush with espresso glaze while they are still hot. Leave the twists to cool on the trays – they will be very delicate at this stage.

15 Once you're ready to enjoy the twists, sprinkle the top of each one with a generous amount of toasted walnut brittle.

Chocolate Glazed Buns

Makes 10 buns
Time Master recipe + 1 day

Batch of *Shokupan* buns (see page 136)
Burned Honey Chocolate Glaze (see page 196)

For the Burned Honey Crème Diplomat

60 g	(2 oz) honey
325 g	(11.5 oz) cream
125 g	(4.4 oz) milk
60 g	(2 oz) egg yolk (about 3 UK medium/ US large eggs)
10 g	(0.4 oz) cornflour (cornstarch)
Pinch of	flaky sea salt, plus extra for sprinkling
1	sheet of gelatine

These buns utilise shokupan bread to maximum effect. Japanese milk bread can carry heaps of filling inside and be topped with numerous combinations of ingredients. This combination was first created around Eastertime but works well all year round.

Day one

1. To make the burned honey crème diplomat, caramelise the honey in a medium saucepan over a medium–high heat until it turns a dark amber colour. It will begin to smoke. Remove the pan from the heat and deglaze the honey with 125 g (4.4 oz) of the cream and the milk.
2. Return the pan to the heat and bring the mixture to below boiling point, whisking to combine the caramelised sugars with the liquids. There might be lumps of 'seized' honey in the cream and milk, but these will melt as you cook out the custard.
3. In a small bowl, whisk together the egg yolk with the cornflour and salt. Pour a little of the just-boiling milk and cream into the egg yolks, whisking quickly and continuously. Transfer the mixture to the pan.
4. Cook the custard out over a low heat until it reaches 85°C (185°F) and is thick, bubbling and smooth. Test with a digital thermometer.
5. Bloom the gelatine in cold water, squeezing out the excess water and whisking it into the hot custard.
6. Place a sieve (fine-mesh strainer) over a small bowl and pass the custard through the sieve to remove any lumps or flecks of honey. Cover with a layer of baking parchment or cling film (plastic wrap) and leave to cool. Once cool, transfer to the refrigerator to set for a minimum of 3 hours and ideally for 24 hours.

Day two

1. Finish making the burned honey crème diplomat by whipping the remaining cream (200 g/7 oz) until soft peaks form. Take the chilled crème diplomat from the refrigerator and beat until smooth and the texture has loosened. Fold the whipped cream through the crème diplomat and transfer to a piping (pastry) bag. Return to the refrigerator.
2. With the point of a sharp knife, create a small hole in the bottom of each bun. Don't pierce all the way through to the other side. Push the point of the knife two thirds of the way into the centre and wiggle it around to make space for the filling.
3. Cut a small opening at the tip of the piping bag and fill each bun with the crème diplomat, using an even pressure while piping. Aim for 45–50 g (1.6–1.8 oz) in each bun. Scrape off any excess with an offset spatula. Once filled, return the buns to the refrigerator.
4. Melt the chocolate glaze in a bain-marie until it is glossy and smooth.
5. Dip the top two thirds of the buns in the glaze, gently shake off the excess and place on a baking tray (pan) lined with baking parchment. Sprinkle with a few flakes of sea salt and enjoy.

Matthew's 'Nduja Buns

Makes 8–10 buns
Time 2 days with Master recipe

Batch of *Shokupan* dough (see page 136)
Hot Honey (see page 196)
Ricotta salata or pecorino, grated
Chervil leaves

For the 'Nduja Béchamel Sauce

1	jar of 'nduja paste (180 g/6.3 oz)
40 g	(1.4 oz) unsalted butter
40 g	(1.4 oz) plain (all-purpose) flour
450 g	(15.8 oz) whole milk
Fine sea salt	

Created for the menu by our bakery manager, Matthew, this recipe is made with a fiery 'nduja béchamel sauce, which is rolled and twisted into shokupan dough. The buns are brushed with *Hot Honey* (see page 196) straight from the oven, then topped with a generous grating of ricotta salata cheese, a drizzle more hot honey and freshly picked chervil for a delicate liquorice hit. They are deliciously soft, spicy, sweet and sticky. Ricotta salata is a firmer version of its creamy counterpart – similar in texture to pecorino or Parmesan.

1. Make the 'nduja béchamel sauce. In a medium saucepan over a low heat, slowly cook out the 'nduja paste, allowing the fats to separate from the pork sausage to create a vibrant red, spicy oil. Using a slotted spoon, scoop out any solids into a small bowl for later.
2. Melt the butter in the same saucepan over a low heat. Mix in the flour and cook out the roux for a couple of minutes. Whisk in the milk and continue cooking over a low heat for 2–3 minutes until the sauce is thick and velvety. Remove from the heat, add the rendered pork sausage and season to taste with sea salt. Store in an airtight container.
3. Remove the dough from the refrigerator and place on a lightly floured surface. Roll the dough out to a larger rectangle, roughly 40 cm (16 in) long and 25 cm (10 in) wide. Ensure the long side of the dough is parallel to you.
4. Spread the béchamel sauce lengthways over two thirds of the dough, then fold the empty third of the dough into the middle and the remaining third over the top, as you would fold a letter. Return the dough to the baking tray (pan), cover with cling film (plastic wrap) and chill in the refrigerator for 30 minutes.
5. Take the dough from the refrigerator and place on a lightly floured work surface. Make sure to rotate the dough, so the open edge of the letter is facing you. Roll the dough into a rectangle using an even pressure until it is 8 mm (½ in) thick.
6. Using a sharp knife or pizza wheel, cut the dough into strips that are 4 cm (1½ in) wide and weigh approximately 100–110 g (3.5–3.9 oz).
7. Roll each strip into a spiral, as you would a Swiss roll (jelly roll), then lay flat on two baking trays lined with baking parchment. Spread the strips out evenly on the trays to give them room to expand.
8. Place the buns in the cold oven to prove for 1½–2 hours – you are using the oven like a proving cabinet. Once proved, the buns should be light and pillowy and will have doubled in size.
9. Remove the buns from the oven. Preheat the oven to 190°C (400°F). Return the buns to the oven, then turn the temperature down to 180°C (390°F) and bake for 14–16 minutes.
10. Once the buns are baked and while they are still hot, brush with the hot honey. Leave to cool on the baking trays.
11. Before serving, grate some ricotta salata or pecorino over the buns. Finely chop the chervil and sprinkle over the top.

Roasted Strawberries and Cream Maritozzi Buns

Makes 12 buns
Time 2 days with Master recipe

Batch of *Shokupan* buns (see page 136)
Icing (confectioners') sugar, for dusting

For the Vanilla Mascarpone Cream

125 g	(4.4 oz) whole milk
½	vanilla pod (bean), seeds and pod
60 g	(2 oz) egg (about 1 UK large egg/US extra-large egg)
30 g	(1 oz) caster (superfine) sugar
12 g	(0.4 oz) cornflour (cornstarch)
1 g	(¼ teaspoon) fine sea salt
15 g	(0.5 oz) unsalted butter (at room temperature)
250 g	(8.8 oz) mascarpone

For the Roasted Strawberries

400 g	(14.1 oz) strawberries, plus around 6 extra to serve
40 g	(1.4 oz) light soft brown sugar

Maritozzis are a weekend staple on our menu. The flavours change on a month-to-month basis, depending on what's in season. What could be better than strawberries and cream? The buns are filled with a vanilla *crème pâtissière* (pastry cream) with added mascarpone.

1 Begin by making the vanilla mascarpone cream. Heat the milk and vanilla pod in a saucepan over a low heat. You don't want the milk to boil – as soon as it begins to steam, remove the pan from the heat.

2 While the milk is heating, whisk together the egg, sugar, cornflour and salt in a small mixing bowl. Pour one third of the milk into the egg mixture and whisk briskly together. Pour the mixture back into the saucepan with the remaining milk.

3 Return the saucepan to a low heat. Whisk for 3–4 minutes until thick and smooth. The mixture should come to a gentle boil and you'll see bubbles and blips on the surface. Remove from the heat and whisk in the softened butter. Pour the vanilla crème pâtissière into an airtight container and refrigerate until you are ready to serve.

4 Next, roast the strawberries. Preheat the oven to 180°C (390°F). While the oven is preheating, wash the strawberries and pat them dry. Remove the green tops and cut the fruits in half. If the strawberries are large, quarter them; if they are small, leave them whole. Put the strawberries and sugar into an ovenproof dish or roasting tin and toss together, coating the fruit evenly with sugar.

5 Roast the strawberries for 30 minutes, checking every 10 minutes and stirring the fruit with the roasting juices. Remove from the oven and set aside to cool.

6 Put the crème pâtissière into a mixing bowl or the bowl of a stand mixer fitted with the paddle attachment. Beat for 1 minute until smooth. In a separate bowl, beat the mascarpone until smooth and free of any lumps.

7 Add the smooth mascarpone cream to the crème pâtissière and beat until you have the texture of thick, velvety cream – about 1 minute.

8 Split the buns in half horizontally, but don't cut them all the way through. Gently open the buns. First, spoon in the roasted strawberries, allowing about 25 g (0.9 oz) of fruit per bun. Let the roasting juices soak into the soft bun. Next, top with a large spoonful of vanilla mascarpone cream. You can also pipe the cream. Close the buns slightly, pushing the soft buns against the cream. Smooth the surface with an offset spatula or a rubber spatula.

9 Dust the buns with a little icing sugar and garnish with half a strawberry. Enjoy within a couple of hours of filling.

COOKIES & BISCUITS

Chocolate Chip and Sea Salt Cookies

Makes 12 large cookies
Time 2 days

---

160 g (5.6 oz) unsalted butter (at room temperature)
200 g (7 oz) caster (superfine) sugar
70 g (2.5 oz) light soft brown sugar
70 g (2.5 oz) Demerara sugar
340 g (12 oz) plain (all-purpose) flour
3 g (1 teaspoon) bicarbonate of soda (baking soda)
4 g (1 teaspoon) baking powder
5 g (¾ teaspoon) fine sea salt
210 g (7.4 oz) dark chocolate (at least 60% cocoa solids) chunks or discs
70 g (2.5 oz) egg (about 1½ UK medium/US large eggs)
Flaky sea salt, for sprinkling

I need to emphasise that these cookies take 24 hours to make. The cookie dough has to rest before baking, otherwise you end up with enormous, flat pancakes that will go incredibly crisp in the oven. What you are aiming for is a cookie with crisp, chewy edges, a soft, chocolatey centre and fudgey notes from a combination of sugars and flaky sea salt to balance. You can keep these cookies in the freezer and bake as needed, which is very helpful in case of emergencies.

Day one

1. Combine the butter and sugars in a stand mixer fitted with the paddle attachment. Cream the butter and sugars together until they are lighter in texture and a pale golden colour. You're not aiming for a fluffy texture here. Scrape down the sides of the mixing bowl to gather any stray pieces of butter or sugar.
2. Whisk together the flour, bicarbonate of soda, baking powder and salt in a large mixing bowl, then add the chocolate pieces.
3. Add the egg to the butter and sugar mixture and beat for 1 minute. Scrape down the sides of the bowl again.
4. Add the flour mixture in three stages on a low speed – you don't want to incorporate air at this stage, but just bring the dough together.
5. Fold the cookie dough several times with a flexible spatula to ensure everything is evenly mixed and distributed. Line two baking sheets with baking parchment.
6. Use a cookie scoop or your hands to weigh out the cookies into 95 g (3.3 oz) balls. Arrange on the baking sheets and cover with cling film (plastic wrap). You now have two options. Put the cookie dough in the refrigerator (it will keep for 3 days) or in the freezer (this will keep for 2 months).
7. Chill the dough for 24 hours before baking. This is really important, as it allows the dough to rest, the sugars to recrystallise and the butter to firm up again, and ultimately the flavour will be better.

Day two

1. When you're ready to bake, preheat the oven to 170°C (375°F). Top the cookies with a generous pinch of flaky sea salt, then bake for 13–14 minutes. If baking from frozen, add an extra minute to the bake time.
2. Remove the cookies from the oven and tap the baking sheets on the work surface. This will knock the air out of the centre of the cookies, creating a soft, fudgey interior.
3. Allow the cookies to cool on the baking sheets before enjoying.

Ginger and Treacle Cookies

Makes 11–12 cookies
Time 1 day

155 g	(5.5 oz) light soft brown sugar
170 g	(6 oz) unsalted butter
50 g	(1.8 oz) egg (about 1 UK large/US extra-large egg)
155 g	(5.5 oz) black treacle (molasses)
310 g	(10.9 oz) plain (all-purpose) flour
11 g	(0.4 oz) bicarbonate of soda (baking soda)
2 g	(½ teaspoon) fine sea salt
5 g	(1 teaspoon) ground cinnamon
2 g	(½ teaspoon) ground ginger
2 g	(½ teaspoon) ground allspice
100 g	(3.5 oz) crystallised ginger, chopped

Demerara sugar, for rolling

These soft, chewy cookies are what I reach for every year when it comes to festive baking. Just before baking, they are rolled in Demerara sugar, which gives the crust an added texture and bite. With rich spicing from ground cinnamon and ground ginger, these are delicious dunked in a mug of tea.

1. Using a stand mixer fitted with the paddle attachment or an electric hand mixer, cream together the sugar and butter until smooth, light and golden in colour.
2. Add the egg in two stages, scraping down the sides of the mixing bowl after each addition. Beat for 2 minutes to incorporate.
3. Next, add the treacle and beat for 1 minute until smooth.
4. Turn down the speed of the mixer and add the flour, bicarbonate of soda, salt, spices and crystallised ginger.
5. Use a cookie scoop or your hands to weigh out the cookies into 80 g (2.8 oz) balls. Arrange on a baking sheet lined with baking parchment.
6. Place the cookies in the freezer until completely frozen. This can take 4–8 hours depending on your freezer.
7. When you're ready to bake, preheat the oven to 180°C (390°F). Line two baking sheets with baking parchment.
8. Remove the cookies from the freezer and roll in Demerara sugar. Space the cookies evenly on the baking sheets.
9. Bake the cookies for 8 minutes, then rotate the baking sheets and bake for a further 8 minutes. Check the cookies – they should have puffed up and feel soft to the touch.
10. Remove the cookies from the oven and give the baking sheets a good, hard tap on the work surface. This will create that quintessential crinkly texture on the outside, while the inside will be soft and chewy.
11. Allow the cookies to cool on the baking sheets. They will keep in an airtight container for a week. The cookie dough balls will last in the freezer for 2 months.

Shortbread with Elderflower Butter

Makes 16 pieces
Time 2 days

For the Elderflower Butter

4	fresh elderflower heads
250 g	(8.8 oz) softened unsalted butter

For the shortbread

Zest of 1 lemon

100 g	(3.5 oz) caster (superfine) sugar, plus extra for sprinkling
200 g	(7 oz) elderflower butter (see above)
300 g	(10.6 oz) plain (all-purpose) flour
5 g	(1 teaspoon) sea salt

This recipe starts with instructions on how to make a compound butter with fresh elderflower. If that is too elaborate for you, you're short on time, or elderflower is no longer in season, you can leave out the compound butter process. This shortbread is a classic recipe of 3:2:1 – three parts flour, two parts butter, one part sugar. Once you remember that ratio, you can whip up shortbread at any time, essentially anywhere. It requires little equipment: just a mixing bowl, wooden spoon and baking tray (pan). Once stored in an airtight container, this shortbread will last for a couple of weeks. The perfect afternoon pick-me-up with a pot of tea.

Day one

1. To make the elderflower butter, wash the elderflowers by placing them in cold water. Pat them dry and use a sharp pair of scissors to cut off all the blooms. The stalks can be bitter.
2. Use a wooden spoon to cream together the butter and flowers in a large mixing bowl. Scrape the butter into an airtight container, so it doesn't oxidise. Leave the butter to infuse for 24 hours at room temperature.

Day two

1. Push the butter through a fine sieve (strainer) and discard the elderflowers. Return the butter to the airtight container.
2. Combine the lemon zest and sugar in a bowl and rub between your fingers for a couple of minutes to release the oils. Add 200 g (7 oz) of the elderflower butter and cream together until smooth.
3. Next, add the flour and salt and bring the ingredients together until they have a breadcrumb texture. Use your hands to squeeze the dough together to form a ball.
4. Tip the dough onto a baking tray (pan) lined with baking parchment, then gently pat it into an even layer. Using your fingertips and palms, press the shortbread into the tray. Press down evenly, pushing the shortbread dough out to the edges. Chill in the refrigerator for 20 minutes. Preheat the oven to 170°C (375°F).
5. Remove the shortbread from the refrigerator and sprinkle with caster sugar. Bake for 25 minutes. The shortbread should look pale and not coloured. Leave to cool for a few minutes before slicing into 16 even squares. Allow to cool completely in the tray before removing, as the shortbread will be very delicate.

Baker's notes

Try blending two flours: using half white spelt flour and half plain (all-purpose) flour results in a shortbread with delicious buttery qualities.

You can also cover the shortbread dough once it has been pressed into the baking tray (pan) with cling film (plastic wrap) or a beeswax wrap and store in the refrigerator for 48 hours before baking.

Anzac Biscuits

Makes 10 small biscuits
Time 30 minutes

75 g	(2.7 oz) rolled oats
45 g	(1.6 oz) desiccated (dried shredded) coconut
50 g	(1.8 oz) plain (all-purpose) flour
45 g	(1.6 oz) wholemeal (whole-wheat) flour
25 g	(0.9 oz) caster (superfine) sugar
25 g	(1 oz) Demerara sugar
20 g	(0.7 oz) light soft brown sugar
2 g	(½ teaspoon) fine sea salt
95 g	(3.4 oz) extra virgin olive oil
30 g	(1 oz) golden (light corn) syrup
15 g	(0.5 oz) water
4 g	(1 teaspoon) bicarbonate of soda (baking soda)

Anzac biscuits (cookies) became popular during World War I when they were supposedly sent overseas to soldiers from the Australian and New Zealand Army Corps because of their nutrient-dense power and long shelf life.

The amazing thing about this recipe is that you can have delicious baked biscuits from start to finish in 30 minutes. We developed these biscuits as a vegan option in the bakery by using extra virgin olive oil as the fat. You can also directly substitute unsalted butter or coconut oil. We also use golden (light corn) syrup to keep the bake vegan-friendly. This can be replaced with honey. I have whipped these biscuits up with a very small newborn strapped to my chest – the recipe requires very little mixing and there's minimal washing up. You only need one mixing bowl and a saucepan. It's a simple recipe for someone new to baking or easy to make if you are tight for time.

1. Preheat the oven to 170°C (375°F) and line two baking sheets with baking parchment.
2. Combine the rolled oats, coconut, two types of flour, three types of sugar and salt in a large mixing bowl.
3. Combine the olive oil, golden syrup and water in a small saucepan. Warm over a low heat until the golden syrup has melted and the mixture is hot. Add the bicarbonate of soda and whisk immediately. The mixture will expand and foam.
4. Pour the oil and syrup mixture into the dry ingredients in the bowl and mix with a flexible spatula or wooden spoon.
5. Weigh out 45 g (1.6 oz) rounds of dough and place on the prepared baking sheets.
6. Bake the biscuits for 12 minutes. They will be delicate when you take them out of the oven, so leave to cool on the baking sheets. The biscuits can be stored in an airtight container for up to a week.

Dried Cranberry and White Chocolate Snickerdoodles

Makes 20 cookies
Time 2 days

150 g	(5.3 oz) unsalted butter
50 g	(1.8 oz) caster (superfine) sugar
125 g	(4.4 oz) light soft brown sugar
75 g	(2.7 oz) egg (about 1½ UK medium/US large egg)
95 g	(3.4 oz) plain (all-purpose) flour
50 g	(1.8 oz) wholemeal (whole-wheat) flour
6 g	(1½ teaspoons) fine sea salt
3 g	(¾ teaspoon) bicarbonate of soda (baking soda)
175 g	(6.2 oz) rolled oats
100 g	(3.5 oz) dried cranberries
100 g	(3.5 oz) white chocolate, chopped

Snickerdoodles are an American staple, a traditional sugar cookie that is commonly tossed in cinnamon sugar before baking. This recipe came about when we were looking for a cookie for ice-cream sandwiches at our market stall during the summer. It needed to be soft and chewy and hold up against melting ice cream. For ice-cream sandwich cookies, leave the dried cranberries and white chocolate out of the recipe. Without the cranberries and white chocolate, you'll have about 16 cookies, but with them you get 20.

Day one

1. Using a stand mixer fitted with the paddle attachment, cream the butter and sugars for 5 minutes until pale and light in texture.
2. Add the eggs in two stages, scraping down the sides and bottom of the bowl as you go.
3. Next, in go the two flours, salt and bicarbonate of soda. Reduce the speed to slow and gently combine the ingredients.
4. Finally, fold through the rolled oats, cranberries and white chocolate. Mix for 1 minute on the slowest speed.
5. Weigh the dough into 45 g (1.6 oz) balls by rolling them gently between your palms. You can wet your hands to make this process easier and less messy.
6. Chill the cookie dough balls for 24 hours before baking. They can be chilled in the refrigerator or in the freezer.

Day two

1. When you're ready to bake, preheat the oven to 180°C (390°F). Line two baking sheets with baking parchment (you may just need one baking sheet).
2. Space the cookies evenly on the baking sheets. They don't spread out a huge amount while baking, but don't overcrowd the sheets. I like to bake eight cookies per baking sheet.
3. Bake cookies chilled in the refrigerator for 14 minutes and frozen cookies for 16 minutes. The centres should be slightly risen and the edges evenly golden.
4. Remove from the oven and tap the baking sheets firmly on the work surface to release the cookies and leave to cool before enjoying.

Sesame and Miso Cookies

Makes 10 cookies
Time 4 hours

75 g	(2.7 oz) smooth tahini
95 g	(3.4 oz) unsalted butter (at room temperature)
140 g	(4.9 oz) light soft brown sugar
60 g	(2 oz) caster (superfine) sugar
10 g	(0.4 oz) shiro miso paste
50 g	(1.8 oz) egg (about 1 UK medium/US large egg)
20 g	(0.7 oz) egg yolk (about 1 UK medium/ US large egg)
200 g	(7 oz) plain (all-purpose) flour
2 g	(½ teaspoon) bicarbonate of soda (baking soda)
1 g	(¼ teaspoon) baking powder
65 g	(2.3 oz) white sesame seeds
15 g	(0.5 oz) black sesame seeds

Al Nakhil tahina extra is my absolute favourite tahini to reach for. It can be found in most Middle Eastern supermarkets and occasionally in delis and independent grocery shops. It's incredibly smooth, never separates and is the best quality. These cookies draw their inspiration from a time-honoured peanut butter cookie, but use tahini paste in its place. They are moreish, with a slightly savoury note from the addition of miso paste. I particularly love the added texture from the sesame seed crust. The cookie dough can be made and baked within the same day.

1. Cream together the tahini, butter, both sugars and the miso paste in a mixing bowl or a stand mixer fitted with the paddle attachment until light in colour – about 2 minutes on a medium speed.
2. Add the egg and egg yolk and beat on a medium speed for a minute, scraping down the sides of the bowl as you go.
3. Next, add the flour, bicarbonate of soda, baking powder and 50 g (1.8 oz) of the white sesame seeds, mixing for a further 30–60 seconds until the mixture is smooth and combined.
4. Weigh the dough into 65 g (2.3 oz) balls. Place on a baking tray (pan) lined with baking parchment, cover with cling film (plastic wrap) and chill in the refrigerator for 3 hours.
5. Once the cookies are chilled, preheat the oven to 180°C (390°F) and line two baking trays with baking parchment.
6. Combine the remaining 15 g (0.5 oz) white sesame seeds and the black sesame seeds in a small bowl. Roll each cookie in the seeds until well coated before placing on the baking trays. Place the trays in the oven and turn the temperature down to 170°C (375°F). Bake the cookies for 14–15 minutes until golden.
7. Remove from the oven and leave the cookies to cool on the baking trays before transferring to an airtight container. The cookies can be stored for up to a week.

Sourdough and Olive Oil Crackers

Makes 6 crackers
Time 1 hour 30 minutes–2 days

---

200 g	(7 oz) leftover levain (see page 95)
60 g	(2 oz) plain (all-purpose) flour, plus extra for dusting
60 g	(2 oz) finely milled wholemeal (whole-wheat) flour
15 g	(0.5 oz) light rye flour
15 g	(0.5 oz) extra virgin olive oil
2 g	(½ teaspoon) fine sea salt

Za'atar or flaky sea salt and dried thyme leaves, for sprinkling

These addictive crackers use sourdough levain discard in the dough. You'll never want to throw out your discard after trying this recipe. The crackers are thin, crisp sheets that you break into bite-size pieces once baked, making a wonderful addition to a cheese board or with dipping bits. It's a really enjoyable process to make these with a pasta machine. If you don't have a pasta machine at home, a rolling pin will do the job – just set aside extra time.

1. Combine all the ingredients in a large mixing bowl and bring together until you have a loose ball of dough.
2. Tip the dough onto a clean work surface and knead for roughly 1 minute until smooth. Flatten the dough into a rough rectangle and wrap tightly with cling film (plastic wrap).
3. Place the dough in the refrigerator to rest for 1–24 hours. Any longer than 24 hours and the dough will become too acidic and won't be as enjoyable to eat.
4. Preheat the oven to 170°C (375°F).
5. Divide the dough into six roughly equal pieces. Flatten the pieces with the palm of your hand and pass through the rollers of a pasta machine. Pass the dough through the widest notch a couple of times to smooth it out and create a uniform texture. Then roll through the notches until the sheets are 2 mm (⅛ in) thick. If rolling out by hand, lightly dust your work surface with flour. Use long, even strokes to roll out each piece of dough. Move the dough around your work surface so it doesn't stick, dusting with more flour if necessary. There will come a stage where you will need to cut the dough into two pieces as they grow in length. You are aiming for crackers that are 7 cm (2¾) wide.
6. Place the thinly rolled pieces of dough on clean, unlined baking trays (pans). Don't let the pieces overlap – I use three baking trays and add two sheets of dough per tray.
7. Next, you can embellish the crackers, depending on how you are going to enjoy them. If you're dipping them in hummus, baba ghanoush and oils, try a sprinkling of za'atar. For a cheese board, go for a generous pinch of flaky sea salt or dried thyme leaves.
8. Bake the crackers for 10–11 minutes. They will shrink and puff up and create little air pockets and bubbles. Remove from the oven and leave to cool before breaking into long shards. Store in an airtight container for up to a week.

FESTIVE BAKES

Christmas Pudding

Makes 3 x 900 g (2 lb)
or 6 x 450 g (15.8 oz) puddings
Time 2 days

180 g	(6.3 oz) Bramley (cooking) apples
170 g	(6 oz) unsalted butter, plus extra for greasing
340 g	(12 oz) dark soft brown sugar
450 g	(15.8 oz) raisins
340 g	(12 oz) sultanas (golden raisins)
115 g	(4.1 oz) *Blood Orange Marmalade* (see page 195) or use shop-bought blood orange marmalade
115 g	(4.1 oz) glacé (candied) cherries
125 g	(4.4 oz) brandy, plus extra for flaming
260 g	(9.2 oz) Guinness
55 g	(1.94 oz) ground almonds
5 g	(1 teaspoon) mixed spice
5 g	(1 teaspoon) ground ginger
5 g	(1 teaspoon) ground cinnamon
5 g	(1 teaspoon) fine sea salt
Zest and juice of 1 lemon	
Zest and juice 1 orange	
115 g	(4.1 oz) plain (all-purpose) flour
225 g	(7.9 oz) fresh sourdough breadcrumbs
250 g	(8.8 oz) egg (about 6 UK medium/US large eggs)

This is a recipe to be passed down to the next generation. A recipe that is timeless and one that I hold very close to my heart. It was given to me by Mimi, who I've mentioned many times in this book. Dating back to 1903, I originally scribbled it down as George III Royal Plum Pudding. Mimi was given this recipe from a dear nun at the Convent of Mercy in Kells, County Meath. I have made very few changes to the original, simply substituting fresh breadcrumbs for sourdough ones and using *Blood Orange Marmalade* (see page 195) instead of mixed peel.

At home, Christmas puddings are made on Stir-up Sunday, which is the last Sunday before Advent. I started practising this tradition with my daughter, Robin, who was born in November.

This is a generous recipe that makes a number of puddings. I suggest you enjoy one yourself and give the others to friends or family – they make the most thoughtful gift, sitting proudly in the centre of anyone's Christmas dessert table.

Day one

1 This recipe will require the largest mixing bowl you have or a large container. Wash the Bramley apples thoroughly and grate them with the skins on.
2 Melt the butter and sugar together until smooth.
3 Combine everything else, except the flour, breadcrumbs and eggs, in the large mixing bowl. Use your hands to evenly distribute the wet ingredients through the dried fruits and spices. Cover the bowl with a dish towel or plate and leave to soak overnight.

Day two

1 Add the flour, breadcrumbs and eggs to the fruit mixture. The mixture will be firmer as the dried fruits absorb the alcohol, sugar and citrus juices. Mix very well, ensuring everything is incorporated and that there are no pockets of flour or breadcrumbs.
2 Grease three 900 g (2 lb) or six 450 g (15.8 oz) pudding bowls with butter, then ladle the pudding mixture into the bowls. Leave 2 cm (¾ in) of space at the tops of the bowls, so the puddings can swell and expand. Cover the tops of the bowls with a double sheet of greaseproof paper, putting a pleat in the fold of the paper to allow the puddings to expand as they steam. Secure with a piece of string.
3 Place each pudding bowl in a large saucepan and add boiling water until it comes halfway up the bowls. Put a lid on the pans (or cover with kitchen foil). Steam the puddings over a low heat for 6 hours.
4 Top up the water, as necessary. You can steam the puddings in batches if you don't have enough saucepans to do them in one go. If you do this, keep the uncooked pudding in the refrigerator until you are ready to steam.

5 Once the puddings are steamed, remove from the saucepans and allow to cool. Leave the baking parchment on top. At this point, the puddings will keep for a year or longer if stored in a cool, dry place. Top up with a tablespoon of brandy every couple of months to keep the fruits plump.

6 You now have two options for preparing the puddings: steaming in the oven or on the hob (stovetop).

To steam in the oven
Preheat the oven to 150°C (350°F). Cover the pudding tightly with kitchen foil and place in a deep roasting tin. Fill the tin with boiling water, 2.5 cm (1 in) from the top, and wrap the tin with foil to form a tight parcel. Steam for 2 hours, then remove and enjoy.

To steam on the hob (stovetop)
Cover the pudding tightly with kitchen foil and place in a heavy-based cooking pot or saucepan. Fill with water until it reaches at least halfway up the pudding bowl. Boil on a low, gentle heat for 2 hours. Top up the pot or pan with water, as necessary.

7 When you are ready to serve your Christmas pudding, flame-warm 3–4 tablespoons of your preferred alcohol (brandy works a treat), pour over the pudding and set alight. Enjoy warm with cold, thick cream or a dollop of *Vanilla Brandy Butter* (see page 175).

Whiskey and Apple Mincemeat

Makes about 1.6 kg (3 lb 8.5 oz) once jarred (enough for about 50 mince pies)

Time 3 hours

---

450 g	(15.8 oz) Bramley (cooking) apples
Zest and juice of 2 lemons	
Zest and juice of 2 oranges	
400 g	(14.1 oz) unsalted butter
240 g	(8.5 oz) dark soft brown sugar
440 g	(15.5 oz) currants
250 g	(8.8 oz) sultanas (golden raisins)
90 g	(3.2 oz) glacé (candied) cherries (optional)
7 g	(1½ teaspoons) mixed spice
7 g	(1½ teaspoons) freshly grated nutmeg
7 g	(1½ teaspoons) ground cinnamon
8 g	(2 teaspoons) ground ginger
100 g	(3.5 oz) Irish whiskey

This is the mincemeat recipe from my childhood and the one we make in the bakery every year. We aim to get it steeping and mingling in October, so the fruits have time soak up the citrus juice and whiskey, becoming deliciously plump. It is heavy on grated Bramley (cooking) apple for added texture and acidity. Growing up in a vegetarian home in the 1990s, this mincemeat – traditionally made with animal suet – was occasionally made with margarine. At home and in the bakery, I use unsalted butter for richness and a subtle savoury undertone. This recipe makes quite a lot of mincemeat, but if you are going the extra mile to make your own, you might as well mix a big batch. It can be jarred and gifted during the festive season.

1. Preheat the oven to 100°C (250°F).
2. Peel and grate the apples and place in a bowl. Sprinkle the citrus zest over the apples, followed by their juices. This will prevent the apples from oxidising and turning brown.
3. Melt the butter and sugar together in a saucepan over a low heat.
4. Add the butter and sugar mixture and all the remaining ingredients except the whiskey with the apples, tossing everything with your hands to coat the fruits evenly in the spices and melted butter. Tip into a deep roasting tin or ovenproof dish.
5. Bake the mincemeat for 1 hour, stirring and rotating the roasting tin every 30 minutes.
6. Remove the mincemeat from the oven and leave to cool. The butter will have pooled in the corners of the tin, so stir occasionally to distribute the fat throughout and coat the fruits. Add the whiskey and stir.
7. Spoon the mincement into sterilised jars (see page 192) or airtight containers. Pack the mincemeat in tightly to remove any air pockets. Press a layer of cling film (plastic wrap) over the mincement to reduce the amount of oxygen getting in. The mincement can be stored in the refrigerator for up to a year.

Vanilla Brandy Butter

Makes 540 g (1 lb 3.5 oz)
Time 30 minutes

220 g	(7.8 oz) icing (confectioners') sugar
1	vanilla pod (bean)
255 g	(9 oz) unsalted butter (at room temperature)
60 g	(2 oz) brandy
5 g	(1 teaspoon) flaky sea salt

An essential accompaniment for mince pies and Christmas pudding, this is our version of the classic recipe with flaky sea salt to balance the sweet Irish butter and speckled with vanilla. In the bakery, we save vanilla pods (sourced from Zazou Emporium) over the course of the year, steeping them in brandy. Come December, we purée the pods in alcohol to create our own vanilla extract. The pods are incredibly fragrant and have plenty of vanilla essence in their skins – it would be wasteful to throw them out. You can also store the pods in a jar of caster (superfine) sugar to use in baking, custards or cream fillings.

1. Sift the icing sugar to remove any lumps. Cut open the vanilla pod lengthways and scrape out all the seeds.
2. Cream the butter, icing sugar and vanilla seeds together in a stand mixer fitted with the paddle attachment on a high speed. Imagine you are making a buttercream here – you want the texture to be incredibly light and airy. This can take up to 10 minutes as you scrape down the sides of the bowl and incorporate any stray pieces of butter.
3. Add the brandy in three or four stages. As you are adding an alcohol to a fat emulsion, it can split on you. So, take care with this stage. Scrape down the sides and bottom of the bowl thoroughly. Keep the mixer on a high speed and cream for a further 3 minutes.
4. Finish the brandy butter with flaky sea salt and spoon into sterilised jars (see page 192) or an airtight container. It will keep for 1 month in the refrigerator.

Whiskey Mince Pies

Makes 12 mince pies
Time 2 days with Master recipe

Batch of *Spelt Flaky Pastry* (see page 58)
15 g (0.5 oz) Demerara sugar
Batch of *Oat Crumble* (see page 75)
360 g (12.7 oz) *Whiskey and Apple Mincemeat* (see page 174) or shop-bought mincemeat

---

Demerara sugar, for sprinkling
Icing (confectioners') sugar and brandy butter, to serve

Baker's note

To make a special individual dessert, serve one of the mince pies warm with a mound of *Marsala-soaked Prunes* (see page 190) and lightly whipped cream.

This recipe requires elements from other recipes in the book. Building recipes and adapting them is one of the most exciting aspects of baking for me.

Our bakery mincemeat is rich and moreish. If you are making our *Whiskey and Apple Mincemeat* (see page 174), you only need a quarter batch. You can also use shop-bought mincemeat instead. I opt for a flaky pastry rather than a buttery shortcrust, as for me this makes for an overwhelming mouthful. Flaky pastry adds a delicate, crumbly crumb and produces a lighter pie.

1. Once the flaky pastry has rested in the refrigerator after its final fold, place it on a lightly floured work surface. Sprinkle the work surface with the Demerara sugar. Roll the pastry out in the sugar into a long rectangle – you are aiming for a thickness of 3–4 mm (¼ in).
2. Cut the pastry into circles with a diameter of 10 cm (4 in). If you want to be precise, you can weigh the discs – each one should weigh about 25–30g (0.9–1 oz). Press the pastry circles into each hole of a 12-hole muffin tin (pan). Fill each pastry case (shell) with 30 g (1 oz) mincemeat. Place in the refrigerator to rest and chill before baking.
3. Don't let the excess pastry go to waste. It can be reused and re-rolled to make more mince pies. Gather up the offcuts of pastry, press them into a rough rectangle and perform one single fold. Cover with cling film (plastic wrap) and return to the refrigerator for a minimum of 30 minutes before rolling out again and cutting more discs.
4. Preheat the oven to 190°C (400°F).
5. While the oven is preheating, take the mince pies and oat crumble topping from the refrigerator. Gently press the crumble into the palm of your hand to form small clumps. Top each mince pie with 25–30g (0.9–1 oz) of crumble. These will bake into the mincemeat as it bubbles on the surface, creating the most deliciously crisp texture.
6. Bake the mince pies in the oven for 5 minutes, then reduce the oven temperature to 180°C (390°F) and bake for a further 20 minutes. Rotate the muffin tin halfway through the baking time if you know your oven has hot spots.
7. The mincemeat can caramelise quickly, making it difficult to remove the mince pies from the tin. So, once the mince pies are baked, remove them immediately from the tin, using an offset spatula to ease them out of the moulds. Leave to cool on a wire rack.
8. Serve the mince pies dusted with icing sugar and enjoy with a generous dollop of brandy butter. Try our homemade *Vanilla Brandy Butter* (see page 175).

Blood Orange Hot Cross Buns

Makes 12 buns
Time 1–2 days

Blood Orange Marmalade (see page 195) or use shop-bought blood orange marmalade
Egg Wash (see page 209)

For the Hot Cross Fruit Mix

110 g	(3.9 oz) *Blood Orange Marmalade* (see page 195) or use shop-bought
50 g	(1.8 oz) boiling water
60 g	(2 oz) currants
60 g	(2 oz) golden raisins (sultanas)
60 g	(2 oz) sultanas (golden raisins)
2 g	(½ teaspoon) freshly grated nutmeg
4 g	(1 teaspoon) ground cinnamon

Pinch of ground all-spice
Pinch of ground cloves

For the Hot Cross Bun Dough

280 g	(9.9 oz) whole milk
50 g	(1.8 oz) egg (about 1 UK medium/US large egg)
7 g	(1½ teaspoons) osmotolerant yeast or 1 sachet of dried active yeast
465 g	(16.4 oz) very strong white bread flour
50 g	(1.8 oz) caster (superfine) sugar
10 g	(0.4 oz) fine sea salt
50 g	(1.8 oz) unsalted butter (at room temperature)

For the Orange Glaze

100 g	(3.5 oz) *Blood Orange Marmalade* (see page 195) or use shop-bought
75 g	(2.7 oz) water
20 g	(0.7 oz) light soft brown sugar

For the Cross Mixture

30 g	(1 oz) plain (all-purpose) flour
30 g	(1 oz) cold water
10 g	(0.4 oz) sunflower oil, plus extra for greasing

Pinch of fine sea salt and sugar

We make these buns every year in the lead up to Easter. They are made with a delicate enriched dough, similar to a brioche, that is studded with dried fruits and spices. Freshly grated nutmeg is a must, as it is more fragrant and aromatic than its dried, powdered counterpart. These buns are exceptional toasted, enjoyed warm with butter and more *Blood Orange Marmalade* (see page 195). You can use shop-bought blood orange marmalade, but ideally make these buns with my homemade version.

1. To make the hot cross fruit mix, purée the blood orange marmalade and boiling water using a hand-held mixer until smooth. Combine all the dried fruits, spices and marmalade purée in a bowl until everything is evenly coated and distributed. Store in an airtight container in the refrigerator for up to 2 months.
2. To make the hot cross bun dough, put the milk, egg and yeast into a stand mixer fitted with the dough hook attachment. Lightly whisk with a fork, then add the flour, sugar and salt. Mix on a medium speed for 8 minutes. Clean down the sides of the bowl with a wet rubber spatula or dough scraper. After 8 minutes the dough should be cleaning the sides of the bowl. If this hasn't happened, mix for another minute.
3. Check the gluten development of the dough by performing the window pane test. To do this, pinch off a small piece of dough and gently stretch it into a square/rectangle between your fingers. Keep stretching until the dough forms a thin film without tearing. You should be able to see through the dough. Continue mixing on a medium speed for another minute if the dough hasn't developed enough to pass this test. Leave the dough to rest for 10 minutes.
4. With the mixer on a medium speed, gradually add the butter. Add a cube at a time, watching as it is incorporated into the dough before adding the next cube. The dough will break apart as you are mixing. It will return to a smooth, even texture after 10 minutes of mixing. Scrape down the edges of the bowl with a wet rubber spatula or dough scraper. Rest for a further 10 minutes.
5. Turn the mixer to medium speed and add the hot cross fruit mix in three stages. Knead for 6–8 minutes. Transfer the dough to a lightly oiled container. Fold the dough over itself – to do this, pull each corner up from the bottom and into the middle. Cover with a dish towel to prevent the dough developing a skin. Leave somewhere warm for 1 hour to prove.
6. While the dough is proving, make the orange glaze. Purée the blood orange marmalade, water and sugar until smooth. Transfer to a small saucepan and bring to the boil for 2 minutes. Remove from the heat and set aside. The glaze can be stored in the refrigerator for up to 2 months in an airtight container.
7. Check the dough and fold it again. Cover and return to somewhere warm for a final 30 minutes of bulk fermentation.

8 After 30 minutes, remove the dough from the oiled container and place on a clean, dry work surface. Divide into 12 balls, each weighing 90 g (3.2 oz). Shape the balls into smooth rounds with the palm of your hand and a dough scraper. Leave to rest for 20 minutes. While the dough balls are resting, line a baking tray (pan) with baking parchment. Round the balls until smooth and place close together on the tray. Leave a 2 cm (¾ in) gap between each bun.

9 Now you have two options. You can either bake the hot cross buns on the same day or keep them in the refrigerator to bake the following morning – if chilling, cover the tray with cling film (plastic wrap) first, making sure there are no gaps for air to get in and create a skin.

To bake the same day

1. Brush the surface of each bun with some egg wash.
2. Place the baking tray in the oven (turned off) with a bowl of water from a recently boiled kettle. The steam will create a warm, humid environment for the buns to rise. Check after 1 hour. The bowl of water may need topping up with freshly boiling water.
3. The buns should have doubled in size – they should be 'kissing' each other's edges and look pillowy and delicate. Prove for a further 30 minutes if they are not there yet.
4. Remove the baking tray from the oven. Preheat the oven to 180°C (390°F).
5. While the oven is preheating, make the cross mixture. Mix everything together in a small bowl and transfer to a piping (pastry) bag. Cut a small opening in the top of the bag. Pipe a line along each row of buns and then repeat in the opposite direction to create the cross.
6. Bake the hot cross buns in the oven for 17–18 minutes. Once baked, brush with the blood orange glaze and allow to cool on the tray.

To bake the next morning

1. Remove the tray from the refrigerator and peel off the cling film. Follow steps 1 to 3 for baking buns on the same day. As these buns are cold from the refrigerator, they will take longer to prove, so after proving for 1 hour, replenish the boiling water and allow to prove for a further 30 minutes.
2. Follow steps 4 to 5 for same-day buns, then bake the hot cross buns for 18–20 minutes. Once baked, brush with the blood orange glaze and allow to cool on the baking tray.

Baker's notes

You need very strong bread flour for this dough. This is important for gluten structure, as you will be adding a large amount of dried fruits and spices, which will impact the overall structure.

The fruit mix can be soaked ahead of time. In the bakery, we start this in early January, when the first of the blood oranges come into season. The glaze can also be made in advance of baking the buns.

Pork, Apple and Mustard Sausage Rolls

Makes 6–7 chunky sausage rolls
Time 2 days with Master recipe

Batch of *Spelt Flaky Pastry* (see page 58)
1 large (extra-large) egg, beaten
Splash of whole milk
Fennel seeds, for sprinkling

For the Pork Filling

35 g	(1.2 oz) finely diced shallot (about 3 shallots)
25 g	(0.9 oz) unsalted butter
Sprig of rosemary or winter savory, finely chopped	
3	big sage leaves, finely chopped
50 g	(1.8 oz) breadcrumbs
1	large Bramley (cooking) apple (about 100 g/3.5 oz)
415 g	(14.6 oz) minced (ground) pork shoulder (the best quality you can find)
30 g	(1 oz) Dijon mustard
8 g	(2 teaspoons) fine sea salt
4 g	(1 teaspoon) freshly ground black pepper
Freshly ground nutmeg	

These sausage rolls will forever and always be associated with Christmas in the bakery. We would make them for the month of December, pulling out all the stops for the monumental Dublin Flea Christmas Market. A cult following ensued and customers still request them to return to the menu on a regular basis. As they appeared on the menu in December, the spices and flavours reflect that time of year: rosemary, nutmeg and a healthy amount of freshly ground black pepper.

1. To make the pork filling, sauté the shallots in a frying pan over a medium heat with the butter, rosemary and sage. Cook for 4–5 minutes until the shallots are translucent and soft. Tip into a medium mixing bowl and add the breadcrumbs. Coat the breadcrumbs with the fragrant melted butter and soft shallots, then leave to cool. Grate the apple with the skin on into a bowl.
2. Once the shallot and breadcrumb mixture is cool, add the minced pork, grated apple, mustard, salt, black pepper, and a good grating of nutmeg. Massage everything together with your hands and work all the ingredients until combined. Cover the bowl with cling film (plastic wrap) or a plate and chill in the refrigerator.
3. On a floured work surface, roll the pastry into a large rectangle, measuring approximately 55 cm (22 in) long and 20 cm (8 in) wide. Move the pastry as you roll, so it doesn't stick to the work surface. Roll with an even pressure until the pastry is about 3 mm (¼ in) thick. Trim any wobbly edges with a knife to keep the rectangle uniform in shape.
4. Form the pork filling into a thick, round log and place along the centre of the rectangle of pastry.
5. Beat the egg with a splash of milk and brush the edges of the pastry. Fold the long side of the pastry over the filling until it meets the opposite side. Run the edge of your hand along the pastry where it meets the filling to push out any air bubbles and to ensure both sides are firmly pressed together.
6. Tidy up the open edge and any excess pastry with a serrated knife. Cut the sausage roll into 7 cm (3 in) lengths.
7. Line a baking tray (pan) with baking parchment and space the sausage rolls evenly on the tray. Brush with more beaten egg and pop in the refrigerator while the oven preheats.
8. Preheat the oven to 200°C (425°F). Brush the sausage rolls with another layer of beaten egg – this will give them a deep golden colour once baked. Sprinkle with fennel seeds.
9. Bake the sausage rolls in the oven for 7 minutes, then reduce the temperature to 180°C (390°F) and bake for a further 15 minutes. The sausage rolls should be puffed up and deep golden and the filling cooked through. You can always check the internal temperature of the pork filling with a digital thermometer.
10. Serve the sausage rolls with a generous dollop of *Tomatillo, Ginger and Chilli Relish* (see page 211) or *Beetroot Jam* (see page 198), or your choice of relish.

Pecan Pie

Makes 1 x 24 cm (9½ in) pie
Time 2 days

For the Chocolate Pastry

55 g	(1.94 oz) unsalted butter (at room temperature)
45 g	(1.6 oz) icing (confectioners') sugar
20 g	(0.7 oz) egg yolk (about 1 UK large/ US extra-large egg)
100 g	(3.5 oz) plain (all-purpose) flour
15 g	(0.5 oz) ground almonds (almond meal)
15 g	(0.5 oz) cocoa (unsweetened chocolate) powder
2 g	(½ teaspoon) fine sea salt

For the Pecan Filling

250 g	(8.8 oz) pecans
105 g	(3.7 oz) unsalted butter
105 g	(3.7 oz) caster (superfine) sugar
150 g	(5.3 oz) light soft brown sugar
45 g	(1.6 oz) brandy
3 g	(¾ teaspoon) fine sea salt
165 g	(5.8 oz) egg (about 4 UK medium/US large eggs)

For the Orange Brandy Cream

250 g (8.8 oz) cream
Zest of 1 orange
Splash of brandy
25 g (0.9 oz) icing (confectioners') sugar

For Thanksgiving one year, our pastry chef at the time, Cissy Difford, developed a pecan pie following a conversation we had about a pie I once made for Thanksgiving dinner in San Francisco that had a rich chocolate crust and a soft-set filling with alcohol and nuts.

Day one

1 To make the chocolate pastry, cream the butter and icing sugar together in a stand mixer fitted with the paddle attachment until smooth and light. You can also use a mixing bowl and wooden spoon.
2 Add the egg yolk and beat until the fats are smooth – about 1–2 minutes. Scrape down the sides and bottom of the bowl.
3 Add the flour, ground almonds, cocoa powder and salt. Bring all the ingredients together until they form a rough ball of dough.
4 Tip the pastry onto a clean work surface and bring together to form one even piece. Flatten the dough into a disc and cover tightly with cling film (plastic wrap). Chill in the refrigerator for 24 hours.

Day two

1 Preheat the oven to 160°C (350°F). Lightly toast the pecans on a baking tray (pan) in the oven for 8 minutes. Once cool, roughly chop – you are looking for a combination of whole pecans, halves and some finer chopped pieces. Set aside.
2 Melt the butter, sugars, brandy and salt in a small saucepan. Allow to cool slightly before mixing in the eggs. The mixture should look smooth and glossy. Set aside.
3 Take the pastry out of the refrigerator and roll between two pieces of baking parchment. Roll out a circle with a diameter of 27 cm (10½ in) that is 4 mm (¼ in) thick. Return the pastry to the refrigerator for 15 minutes to chill and firm up.
4 Preheat the oven to 180°C (390°F). Line a 24 cm (9½ in) tart tin (pan) with the pastry. Drape the pastry over the tin and press it firmly into the edges and bottom. Line with baking parchment and then fill with baking beans (pie weights). Scrunch up the paper beforehand to make it easier to push into the pastry edges for an even blind bake.
5 Blind bake the pastry case for 15 minutes. Remove the paper and baking beans and return the blind-baked pastry shell to the oven for a further 3 minutes. Remove from the oven.
6 Turn the oven temperature down to 160°C (350°F).
7 Add the toasted pecans to the pastry case, then ladle over the filling. Depending on the depth of the tart tin, you might have a small amount of filling left over. My pie held a total of 450 g (1 lb) of filling. Bake the pie for 22 minutes, then check the centre. I added an additional 2 minutes to get the right jiggle – you want the centre to have a wobble to it. Allow to cool before serving.
8 To make the orange brandy cream, whisk together the cream, orange zest, brandy and icing sugar until soft and thick. Serve each slice of pecan pie with a generous dollop of cream.

LARDER

Infused Oils

Makes 300 g (10.6 oz)
Time 2 days

200 g	(7 oz) unblanched leaves, such as fig, lemon verbena or blackcurrant
400 g	(14.1 oz) neutral oil, such as sunflower or grapeseed oil

This method is inspired by Anna Higham's book *The Last Bite*. Infusing oils is an excellent technique to have in your repertoire for capturing a flavour at its peak – use it in the moment or store in the freezer. Our go-to infusions use fig leaves, lemon verbena, blackcurrant leaves and sweet woodruff. The same method can be applied to chives, the green tops of leeks, lovage, mint, and so on. Scale the ingredients up or down to suit your requirements. Follow a ratio of one part leaf to two parts oil. Delicious flavour combinations include fig leaf oil with raspberries, lemon verbena oil with blackberries, and blackcurrant oil with blackcurrants.

Fig leaf oil is used in our *Raspberry and Fig Leaf Danish* (see page 47). For the best flavour, select young, glossy fig leaves. I find that the mature leaves lose their intensity over the growing season. Keep in mind that fig trees are deciduous and will shed their leaves seasonally, usually around the first frost after autumn. Always wash the leaves before cooking with them.

Day one

1. Wash and pat dry the leaves or herbs. Bring a large pot of water to the boil and blanch the leaves until tender (about 30–60 seconds), then refresh them in iced water.
2. Drain off any excess water by squeezing the blanched leaves in a dish towel or piece of muslin (cheesecloth).
3. Use a high-powered upright blender to blitz the oil and blanched leaves for 10 minutes on a high speed. The oil will heat up as you are blending due to the friction and speed. The pulp will separate from the oil, producing an incredibly green, vibrant liquid.
4. Place a sieve (fine-mesh strainer) lined with muslin over a bowl or container. Pour the oil into the sieve and leave to strain in the refrigerator overnight. Don't squeeze or push the pulp through as this will make the oil cloudy.

Day two

Store the strained oil in an airtight container or freeze. It will keep in the refrigerator for 2 weeks and in the freezer for 6 months.

Marsala-soaked Prunes

Makes 1 large Kilner jar (capacity about 2 kg/4 lb 8 oz)
Time 2 days

1	lemon
1	orange
200 g	(7 oz) caster (superfine) sugar
750 g	(1 lb 10 oz) water
2	cinnamon sticks
2	vanilla pods (beans), halved and seeds removed
1 kg	(2 lb 4 oz) Agen prunes, or the best quality you can find
4	breakfast tea bags
250 g	(8.8 oz) Marsala

These prunes are pretty fabulous and can be served with crème fraîche or sweetened mascarpone. You can purée the soaked prunes and syrup to make a luscious base for a Bakewell tart or to fold through a rich chocolate cake mix. Or enhance a rice pudding by placing a couple of these prunes on top along with a drizzle of syrup. They are also excellent eaten alone. At Christmas, I like to enjoy them alongside a warm mince pie and cold, cold pouring cream. Don't forget about the syrup – it's almost the best bit. Thick, dark and aromatic.

Day one

1. Remove the peel of the lemon and orange and juice both fruits. Place both juice and peel in a large saucepan.
2. Next, add the sugar, water, cinnamon sticks and vanilla pods and seeds to the pan. Place over a medium heat and bring to the boil.
3. Once the syrup has boiled, remove the pan from the heat before adding the prunes. Submerge the prunes in the syrup along with the tea bags. Leave the tea bags on the surface, so they are easy to fish out later.
4. Cover the pan with the lid and leave to soak for 24 hours.

Day two

1. Remove the cinnamon sticks, lemon and orange peel and tea bags. Pour in the Marsala and mix to incorporate into the syrup. Be gentle, as the prunes will be plump and delicate.
2. Pour everything into a sterilised jar (see page 192) and seal tightly. These soaked prunes will improve with age. I recommend leaving everything to mingle for a couple of days before enjoying. They can be stored for up to a year.

Rhubarb Compote

Makes 1 x 1 kg (2 lb 4 oz) container
Time 2 hours–2 days

750 g	(1 lb 10 oz) rhubarb
450 g	(15.8 oz) caster (superfine) sugar
25 g	(0.9 oz) lemon juice
12 g	(0.4 oz) citric acid

The weight of sugar to fruit in this recipe is lower than in a jam: 60 per cent sugar to chopped rhubarb. The result is a tangier compote with a looser texture. The subtle flavours of the rhubarb shine through. The addition of citric acid is to help retain the vibrant pink colour, but you can leave this out if you wish. We make large batches of this at a time – this is a reduced amount of our recipe, so feel free to double or triple it for your own larder. Don't go bigger than 2.25 kg (5 lb) of fruit in the saucepan as it will take longer to boil and this will impact the final colour.

1. Wash the rhubarb stalks and dice into 2 cm (¾ in) pieces. Cover the rhubarb with the sugar and lemon juice in a large mixing bowl, then leave to steep for a minimum of 1 hour or ideally overnight. Steeping will speed up to the cooking process and improve colour retention.
2. Put all the ingredients into a preserving pan or heavy-based saucepan and place over a low heat. Stir until the sugar has dissolved. Once the sugar has dissolved, increase the heat. Rhubarb contains a high volume of water, so the compote will splatter as it boils. Watch out for your hands, wrists and forearms – it can be volcanic if it hits your skin.
3. Boil the mixture until it reaches a temperature of 103–105°C (217–221°F), the liquid has reduced and the compote is thick and glossy. Use a digital thermometer to check the temperature. Stir continuously, as the fibres of the rhubarb can stick to the bottom of the saucepan and burn.
4. Pour the rhubarb compote into an airtight container and allow to cool before transferring to the refrigerator, where it will keep for 5 days.

Notes on Jam

For me, jams (jellies) reflect a moment in time. You are capturing the fruit at its peak and preserving it for another part of the year. For jamming, I use fresh fruit that is just ripe. You can also use frozen fruits – they are often high quality as they are picked at their best and frozen immediately. If using frozen fruits, you may find they break down and come to the boil faster than their fresh counterparts. This is because the freezing process can break down the skins and cell walls within the fruit.

I've included three jam recipes in this chapter, which all follow the same principle: 75 per cent sugar to the weight of the fruit. A lot of recipes in the jam-making world will call for equal parts sugar to fruit. For me, that produces a jam that is too cloyingly sweet. You want the brightness and flavour of the fruit to shine. By reducing the sugar weight to three quarters of the fruit, you are still able to achieve a firm set and long shelf life on the jarred item. I use caster (superfine) sugar for my jams but you can also use granulated.

If I was to recommend two pieces of kit for jam-making it would be a preserving saucepan and a digital thermometer. A preserving saucepan is conical in shape, allowing for really efficient water evaporation, resulting in your jam boiling and reaching setting point faster. This will help with retaining the vibrancy in colour and flavour. A digital thermometer will give you an accurate temperature for when you reach setting point.

It can be tempting to make large batches of jam in one go, but I have a rule of no more than 2.5 kg (5 lb 8 oz) of fruit in the saucepan at a time. From years of experience I have found that anymore than that means the jam will boil for a prolonged length of time, dulling the flavour and colour of the fruits.

Notes on marmalade

The process of marmalade can't be rushed, so choose a day when you don't have much planned or anywhere to hurry off to.

I opt for the 'sliced-fruit method' rather than the 'whole-fruit method' for most of the marmalades I make in the bakery. I've had great success making grapefruit, bergamot and lemon marmalades with this technique. However, I avoid this method for citrus with a thicker peel such as Seville oranges. Blood oranges have a thin, tender peel, which doesn't need hours of poaching before jamming begins.

First, the citrus is shredded and placed in cold water along with its juices. Soaking the citrus helps to release the pectin from the peels. They also soften in the water, reducing the length of the poaching stage. Ideally, the fruit is left to soak for a minimum of 24 hours.

Decide on your desired texture for the marmalade in advance: thick cut or finely shredded. I aim for something in the middle as I want the finished marmalade to be spreadable but still have a 'bite' to it. I also like to season marmalade with a small amount of sea salt. It amplifies the flavours and balances the bitter and sweet notes.

How to sterilise jars

Sterilising is an important step to remove any potential yeasts or bactaria that may spoil your hard work. If you are using a jam funnel and ladle to fill your jars, I'd suggest washing them, too.

1. Preheat the oven to 160°C fan (350°F).
2. Wash the jars and lids in very hot, soapy water and rinse well.
3. If the jars you are using have rubber seals, remove those and wash well, too.
4. Dry the jars and lids on a wire rack in the oven for 10 minutes.
5. Remove from the oven.
6. Fill the jars while they are still warm and screw the lids on tightly.
7. You can also use sterilising solution or tablets – simply follow the manufacturer's directions.

Raspberry Jam

Makes 5–6 x 220 g (7.8 oz) jars
Time 1 hour 40 minutes

1 kg	(2 lb 4 oz) fresh or frozen raspberries
750 g	(1 lb 10 oz) caster (superfine) sugar
50 g	(1.8 oz) lemon juice (about 1 lemon)

1. Put the raspberries, sugar and lemon juice into a preserving pan or large, heavy-based saucepan. If possible, leave to sit for 1 hour to macerate, as this will help the sugar dissolve.
2. Bring the raspberries and sugar to a gentle simmer over a low heat. Using a wooden spoon, make sure to stir and dissolve all the sugar. Do not increase the heat until the sugar has dissolved completely.
3. Increase the heat and bring to a rapid boil. Raspberry jam can reach its setting point very quickly, so keep an eye on it while it boils. Stir continuously, as the seeds can catch on the bottom of the pan.
4. Cook to 104–105°C (219–221°F), using a digital thermometer to check the temperature.
5. Pour the jam into warm, sterilised jars (see page 192) and seal immediately with tight-fitting lids. Store in a cool, dark place. The raspberry jam will keep for 6 months. Once opened, store in the refrigerator.

Apricot Jam

Makes 3 x 220 g (7.8 oz) jars
Time 2 days

475 g	(16.7 oz) apricots (about 10 apricots)
350 g	(12.4 oz) caster (superfine) sugar
50 g	(1.8 oz) lemon juice (about 1 lemon)

Day one

1. Cut the apricots in half and remove the stones. Cut each apricot half into 6–8 pieces. Don't throw the stones away.
2. Put the apricot pieces, caster sugar and lemon juice into a mixing bowl, toss the fruit between your hands and cover with a plate or cling film (plastic wrap). Leave somewhere cool to macerate for 24 hours.

Day two

1. Put the macerated apricots into a preserving pan or heavy-based saucepan, then bring to a rapid boil over a high heat, stirring constantly as the skins of the apricots can stick the bottom of the pan.
2. Boil the jam for 10–12 minutes until it reaches 105°C (221°F) on a digital thermometer.
3. Pour the jam into warm, sterilised jars (see page 192) and seal immediately with tight-fitting lids. Store in a cool, dark place. The apricot jam will keep for 6 months. Once opened, store in the refrigerator.

Blackcurrant Jam

Makes 5–6 x 220 g (7.8 oz) jars
Time 1 hour 40 minutes

1 kg	(2 lb 4 oz) fresh or frozen blackcurrants
750 g	(1 lb 10 oz) caster (superfine) sugar
50 g	(1.8 oz) water

Put the blackcurrants, sugar and water into a preserving pan or large, heavy-based saucepan, then follow the instructions in steps 1 to 5 for making and storing *Raspberry Jam* (see page 194).

Blood Orange Marmalade

Makes 6 x 220 g (7.8 oz) jars
Time 2 days

750 g	(1 lb 10 oz) blood oranges (about 3 large or 6 smaller oranges), washed, stalks removed and cut in half
1 kg	(2 lb 4 oz) water
50 g	(1.8 oz) lemon juice (about 1 lemon)
750 g	(1 lb 10 oz) caster (superfine) sugar
5 g	(1 teaspoon) fine sea salt

Day one

1. Slice the oranges into 3–4 mm (¼ in) half-moons, place in an airtight container or large bowl and cover with the water. Leave in the refrigerator for 24 hours.

Day two

1. Chill a couple of small plates in the freezer.
2. Transfer the oranges and water to a preserving pan or heavy-based saucepan.
3. Add the lemon juice to the pan. Place over a medium heat and bring to simmering point. Poach the slices until the peel breaks between your fingers and feels tender to the touch. This could take 45–90 minutes.
4. Once the orange slices are tender, add the sugar, stirring to fully dissolve. Increase the heat to high and bring to a rolling boil. Boil for 15–25 minutes until the marmalade has reached setting point –105°C (221°F) on a digital thermometer.
5. To check you have the desired set for the marmalade, spoon a small amount onto the chilled plate. Push your finger through the marmalade – you want it to wrinkle and not flood back in to fill the gap. If you don't have the right consistency, boil for a further 5 minutes.
6. Remove the marmalade from the heat, add the sea salt and leave to stand for 10 minutes. This allows the peel to distribute evenly and stops it sinking to the bottom of the jar.
7. Pour into warm, sterilised jars (see page 192) with tight-fitting lids and seal immediately. Store in a cool, dark place. The marmalade will keep for 6 months. Once opened, store in the refrigerator.

Whiskey Caramel Sauce

Makes 6 x 220 g (7.8 oz) jars
Time 30 minutes

140 g	(5 oz) light soft brown sugar
200 g	(7 oz) unsalted butter, cubed
1 x 397 g	(14 oz) tin of condensed milk
5 g	(1 teaspoon) ground ginger
5 g	(1 teaspoon) fine sea salt
150 g	(5.3 oz) Irish whiskey

This thick, boozy sauce is very naughty. You can dollop it on top of brownies, swirl it through vanilla ice cream or enjoy it on warm porridge (oatmeal). Or, try enhancing your Irish coffee game with a couple of spoonfuls in your espresso. This is something we sell in the bakery during the festive season. It makes a lovely homemade gift or a stocking filler for family and friends. Did someone mention espresso martinis ...

1. It's important to use a heavy-based saucepan to make this sauce. First, melt the sugar in a saucepan over a medium heat for 10 minutes until it has caramelised. I use a wooden spoon for this job to get into all the corners of the pan.
2. Once the sugar is a deep caramel colour, add the cubed butter and whisk. Note that the mixture can separate if the butter is very cold.
3. Reduce the heat to low and add the condensed milk, ginger and salt. Make sure you're scraping down the sides of the pan as you incorporate the condensed milk into the caramel.
4. Remove the pan from the heat and carefully pour the whiskey into the sauce in three stages, then blend with a hand-held blender to emulsify until the sauce has a smooth and silky texture.
5. If you are giving the sauce away as gifts, pour into warm sterilised jars (see page 192) and seal tightly. Alternatively, you can store in an airtight container. The sauce will keep in the refrigerator for 1 month.

Burned Honey Chocolate Glaze

Makes 300 g (10.6 oz)
Time 30 minutes

85 g	(3 oz) honey
80 g	(2.8 oz) cream
15 g	(0.5 oz) unsalted butter
25 g	(0.9 oz) light soft brown sugar
12 g	(0.4 oz) cocoa (unsweetened chocolate) powder
85 g	(3 oz) dark chocolate
Pinch of fine sea salt	

This glaze has a wonderful sheen, which makes it perfect for finishing pastries and bakes. Try using it for our *Chocolate Glazed Buns* (see page 146) and *Éclairs with Milk Chocolate and Olive Oil* (see page 70). It's also a great recipe to have in your repertoire to use as a chocolate sauce for drizzling over ice cream, serving with profiteroles or topping pancakes. For this recipe, use a generic blended honey that is mild and less complex in flavour. You can also opt out of the burned honey flavour by using a good-quality honey from your local farmers' market and skipping the caramelisation stage.

1. In a small saucepan over a low heat, heat the honey until it is bubbling and has deepened in colour. The honey will bubble and foam. Stir the honey as it heats for 3 minutes. After about 3 minutes, the honey will start to smoke.
2. Remove the pan from the heat and add the cream. The cream will splatter, so watch your hands and arms. Whisk continuously until the honey and cream have combined.
3. Next, add the butter, sugar and cocoa powder. Change from a whisk to a rubber spatula and carefully bring all the ingredients together. You may need to return to a low heat to ensure everything melts together.
4. Remove the pan from the heat and add the dark chocolate, stirring until you have a smooth, glossy sauce.
5. Use the sauce immediately or keep in the refrigerator in an airtight container.

Hot Sauce

Makes 1 x 200 g (7 oz) jar
Time 7 days

150 g	(5.3 oz) red chillies
10	peppercorns, crushed
2	cardamom pods, crushed
50 g	(1.8 oz) garlic cloves (about 4 cloves), peeled
30 g	(1 oz) fine sea salt
360 g	(12.7 oz) water
30 g	(1 oz) sugar

1 Sterilise a large jar (see page 192) – the jar must have a spring-loaded lid to allow gas and air bubbles to release as the hot sauce ferments.
2 Cut the chillies in half, then deseed them and remove the white veins. If you love hot heat, leave the seeds in.
3 Put the chillies, crushed peppercorns, cardamom pods and garlic into the jar.
4 Next, add the salt, water and sugar. Close the clasp tightly on the jar and gently shake to help the sugar and water to dissolve.
5 Weigh down the ingredients with a small plate or bowl, so the chillies are submerged in the water.
6 Leave the jar in a cool, dry spot in your kitchen for a week. Every day, 'burp' the jar to release any gas that is building up. This is a really important step.
7 After a week, the liquid will have fermented, developing a strong, garlicy punch. Pour the contents into a food processor and blitz until smooth and vibrant in colour.
8 Store the hot sauce in the refrigerator, as this will slow down/halt the fermentation process. It will keep in the refrigerator for 3 months.

Hot Honey

Makes 300 g (10.6 oz)
Time 30 minutes

200 g	(7 oz) honey
50 g	(1.8 oz) apple cider vinegar
50 g	(1.8 oz) fresh ginger, skin on and thinly sliced
2	garlic cloves, peeled and crushed
1–2	red chillies, sliced thinly with seeds
2 g	(½ teaspoon) dried chilli (hot pepper) flakes

I have followed a 4:1 recipe for this hot honey *agrodolce*. If you would like it slightly more acidic, add another splash of vinegar to taste. Gauge your spice tolerance, too: if you like things hot and spicy, add two chillies; if you're on the milder end of the spice spectrum, add just one. We use this hot honey in the bakery to glaze soft brioche 'nduja buns (see page 149). At home, it is our go-to for pizza night – inspired by Bambino Dublin's hot honey, which is drizzled over their pepperoni pizza slices. Don't use expensive, floral honey for this recipe as it'll be lost among the chilli and garlic. Reach for a runny organic honey from the supermarket instead.

1 Combine all the ingredients in a medium saucepan over a medium heat. Boil rapidly for 3 minutes. Remove from the heat and leave to stand for 15 minutes to infuse.
2 Check the heat and acidity levels and adjust as necessary.
3 Strain the hot honey into a sterilised jar (see page 192) and seal with a tight-fitting lid. The hot honey will keep for 6 months.

Beetroot Jam

Makes about 3 x 200 g (7 oz) jars
Time 2 hours

1 kg	(2 lb 4 oz) purple, red, yellow or white beetroots (beets)
200 g	(7 oz) caster (superfine) sugar
100 g	(3.5 oz) lemon juice (about 3 lemons)
Zest of 1 lemon	
Zest of 1 lime	
Knob of ginger, peeled and grated	
5 g	(1 teaspoon) fine sea salt

This jam (jelly) is adapted from Pam Corbin's book *Pam the Jam* along with my mum's personal tweaks. My mum has an enviable jam cupboard that she tops up throughout the year and she is known for giving jars to friends and family instead of a bottle of wine. This jam is best made in late summer or early autumn when beetroots (beets) are at their best.

1. Preheat the oven to 180°C (390°F). Wash the beetroots thoroughly and trim off the tops, if necessary. Wrap the beetroots individually in kitchen foil and place in a roasting tin. Roast in the oven for about 40 minutes. Alternatively, you can simmer the beetroot in a large saucepan of water for 20–25 minutes.
2. Remove the beetroots from the oven and leave to cool before rubbing off the skins. You can do this with your hands or a dish towel (as long as you don't mind this getting stained).
3. Grate the beetroot, then place in a large preserving pan or heavy-based saucepan with the sugar, lemon juice, lemon and lime zests, ginger and salt. Leave everything to macerate for a minimum of 30 minutes.
4. Place the pan over a medium heat and bring the ingredients to a simmer. Cook for 20 minutes, or until the liquids have evaporated and the mixture is thick.
5. Spoon the jam into warm sterilised jars (see page 192), tapping these gently on the work surface to remove any air pockets. Seal the jars tightly. Pam recommends sealing the jars in a water bath for 5 minutes.
6. Once opened, the beetroot jam should be kept in the refrigerator and used within 2 weeks.

Mojo Verde

Makes 350 g (12.4 oz)
Time 10 minutes

60 g	(2 oz/large bunch) coriander (cilantro)
4	garlic cloves, crushed
1	green chilli, seeds removed
15–	(0.5–0.7 oz) apple
20 g	cider vinegar
1.5 g	(½ teaspoon) ground cumin
80 g	(2.8 oz) extra virgin olive oil
Flaky sea salt	

This vibrant green sauce works wonderfully with grilled white fish or griddled green beans, stirred through pasta or poured over ricotta as a dip.

1. Wash and pat dry the coriander leaves. For this recipe, you need both the leaves and stalks.
2. Pulse all the ingredients together in a food processor before blending until smooth and vibrant green.
3. Store in an airtight container. It will keep in the refrigerator for 3 days.

Bread and Butter Pickles

Makes 600 g (1 lb 5 oz)
Time 1 hour 30 minutes

225 g	(7.9 oz) courgette (zucchini), thinly sliced (about 3 small courgettes)
60 g	(2 oz) white onion (about 1 onion), thinly sliced
10 g	(0.5 oz) fine sea salt
170 g	(6 oz) apple cider vinegar
65 g	(2 oz) caster (superfine) sugar
1	teaspoon mustard seeds
1	teaspoon mustard powder
4 g	(1 teaspoon) ground turmeric
115 g	(4.1 oz) water

1. Put the courgette and onion into a medium bowl with the salt, cover with iced water and leave for 1 hour.
2. While the courgette and onion are in water, you can make the pickle vinegar. Bring the vinegar, sugar, spices and water to the boil in a saucepan. Leave to cool.
3. Drain the courgette and onion and pat dry, then transfer to a sterilised jar (see page 192) and pour over the cold vinegar. Place in the refrigerator and enjoy within a week.

Walnut Miso Crunch

Makes 500 g (1 lb 5 oz)
Time 40 minutes

220 g	(7.8 oz) walnuts
120 g	(4.2 oz) sunflower oil
3	garlic cloves, very thinly sliced (ideally on a mandoline)
60 g	(2 oz) sesame oil
30 g	(1 oz) shiro miso paste
30 g	(1 oz) honey
30 g	(1 oz) tamari

1. Preheat the oven to 170°C (375°F). Place the walnuts on a baking tray (pan) and toast in the oven for 8 minutes. Keep an eye on the walnuts, as they will burn very easily and the skins can become incredibly bitter if they go too far. Remove the walnuts from the oven and run a knife through them to break them up into coarse pieces.
2. Heat the sunflower oil to 120°C (250°F) in a medium saucepan.
3. Place a sieve (fine-mesh strainer) over a metal bowl. Fry the garlic in the oil until golden brown, then immediately strain the slices out of the oil.
4. Let the oil cool slightly before adding the toasted walnuts, sesame oil, miso paste, honey, tamari and fried garlic. Mix everything together thoroughly. Allow to cool before serving. Store in an airtight container or jam jar with a tight-fitting lid – the crunch can be stored for 1 month.

Vanilla Marshmallows

Makes 40 small or
15 large marshmallows
Time 2 days

90 g	(3.2 oz) egg white (about 3–4 UK medium/ US large eggs)
8	gelatine sheets
200 g	(7 oz) caster (superfine) sugar
100 g	(3.5 oz) liquid glucose
65 g	(2 oz) water
1	vanilla pod (bean)
100 g	(3.5 oz) icing (confectioners') sugar
30 g	(1 oz) cornflour (cornstarch)

Neutral oil such as sunflower or groundnut (peanut) oil, for greasing

These are squidgy, soft, pillowy marshmallows that we serve alongside our hot chocolate (see opposite). We developed the recipe so the marshmallows slowly melt in the heat of the warm, chocolatey milk. We cut them into large squares, but feel free to cut them smaller to scatter over the top of your drink.

Day one

1. Whisk the egg whites in a stand mixer fitted with the whisk attachment until medium peaks form. While the egg whites are whipping, soften the gelatine sheets in cold water.
2. Combine the sugar, liquid glucose and water in a small saucepan over a medium heat and bring to 121°C (250°F) – use a digital thermometer to measure the temperature.
3. Remove the pan from the heat, squeeze the excess water from the bloomed gelatine sheets and add immediately to the sugar syrup. Stir until the gelatine has dissolved.
4. Increase the speed on the stand mixer. Once the egg whites are at a stiff peaks, begin to slowly pour the sugar syrup into the bowl. Pour a steady stream down the side of the bowl rather than into the centre on top of the whisk attachment. Whip until the mixture is glossy, thick, smooth and shiny.
5. Scrape all the seeds from the vanilla pod and add them to the marshmallow mixture. Continue to whip on high. The addition of the vanilla can deflate the mixture slightly. Whip for a total of 5 minutes.
6. While the marshmallow is whipping, grease a baking tray (pan) with oil.
7. Pour the mixture into the prepared baking tray – it will still be hot at this stage and easy to spread. Level the surface with an offset spatula. Brush a piece of baking parchment with oil and smooth it over the surface of the marshmallow to prevent a hard skin developing. Leave to set for a minimum of 2 hours and ideally overnight.

Day two

1. Sift the icing sugar and cornflour into a bowl and set aside. Peel off the baking parchment from the marshmallow and dust the surface with the icing sugar/cornflour mixture.
2. Run a spatula or sharp paring knife around the edge of the baking tray to release the sides of the marshmallow. Flip the tray over and gently shake until you hear the marshmallow release from the sides. Dust the surface with more of the icing sugar/cornflour mixture.
3. Cut the large marshmallow into your desired shapes. As you are cutting each row, dust over more icing sugar/cornflour mixture to stop the edges sticking together. For our hot chocolates we go big, cutting 5 cm (2 in) cubes. Toss the cut marshmallows in the remaining icing sugar/cornflour mixture before storing them in an airtight container. Store in single layers, separated by baking parchment. They will keep for a week.

Jeff's Hot Chocolate Powder

Makes enough for 20 large mugs
Time 20 minutes

250 g	(8.8 oz) Demerara sugar
75 g	(2.7 oz) cocoa (unsweetened chocolate) powder
3 g	(¾ teaspoon) fine sea salt
500 g	(1 lb 2 oz) dark chocolate (at least 80% cocoa solids), finely chopped

Baker's note

To add texture to your hot chocolate, pour it into a large cafetière and pump it several times. This will create a microfoam and give it a silky, delicious texture similar to steaming it with an espresso machine.

This delicious hot chocolate was developed by our general café manager, Jeff. We knew we wanted to have an in-house hot chocolate blend that was rich, silky and perfect with whole milk or oat milk. Fine-tuned over many weeks and through taste tests with very eager customers, we think it's pretty perfect. Many different variations and iterations later, Jeff landed on Demerara sugar for caramelly notes. Note that the recipe includes sea salt, which really helps balance the final drink.

1. Put the sugar, cocoa powder and salt into a food processor. Blitz until the mixture resembles brown, powdered sugar. This fine consistency makes it super easy to melt when you make hot chocolate. It also prevents the chocolate clumping on the blades of the food processor.
2. Add half the chopped chocolate to the food processor. Gradually blend the ingredients in pulses. You don't want the processor to get hot, as this will melt the chocolate. Add the remainder of the chocolate and pulse until you have a consistent powder.
3. Store the hot chocolate powder in an airtight container or jar with a tight-fitting lid. It will keep for 6 months.

Making a hot chocolate

1. If you have an espresso machine with a steam wand, combine 180 g (6.3 oz) milk and 40 g (1.4 oz) chocolate powder in the milk jug (pitcher) and steam together.
2. If you don't have an espresso machine, pour 300 g (10.6 oz) milk into a small saucepan and heat until it reaches 70°C (150°F). Use a digital thermometer to measure the temperature. Overheating the milk will result in a loss of its natural sweetness. Once you hit the right temperature, add 40 g (1.4 oz) of your homemade chocolate powder and, while whisking, maintain a temperature of about 70°C (150°F) until all the powder has dissolved and the milk is smooth and silky. Serve in your favourite mug with a dusting of chocolate powder and our *Vanilla Marshmallows* (see opposite).

OPENHIVE HONEY Conservation is at the heart of OpenHive Honey. It was started in 2019 by three friends, Kyle Petrie, Mark Earley and Jack McGrath, as a conservation organisation to rear and breed the native Irish black honeybee. Their goal is to help this honeybee re-establish in the Irish ecosystem with as little impact to the local environment and biodiversity as possible and with minimal intervention. To support their efforts, the guys sell locally produced raw Irish honey from apiaries in Dublin, Wicklow and Galway. Every jar sold supports the native Irish honeybee.

The closest apiary to the bakery is 6 km (3.7 miles) away, nestled in the Glen of the Downs nature reserve, a dense oak woodland with native Irish species of cherry, rowan and ash. The glen itself is a Special Area of Conservation protected by the EU. The honey we use at Scéal can be traced to the very hive it came from. Every jar is specific to the place where the bees have foraged for that honey, with the flavour, texture, aroma and complexity changing as the seasons shift. No two apiaries will produce the same flavour of honey; all of them are unique to their surroundings. Here in north Wicklow, nectar and pollen start with dandelions at the beginning of spring, move to clover, heather and rapeseed in the height of summer, then towards brambles and ivy in early autumn before the bees turn to hibernation.

I have fond memories of smothering my *Granny's Brown Bread* (see page 134) with lots of Irish butter and honey.

ASLAMCO

Brandy Syrup

Makes 350 g (12.4 oz)
Time 15 minutes

150 g	(5.3 oz) water
150 g	(5.3 oz) caster (superfine) sugar
50 g	(1.8 oz/3½ tablespoons) brandy

This syrup is used for our *Twice-baked Almond Croissants* (see page 35).

1 Combine the water and sugar in a small, heavy-based saucepan. Whisk to ensure the sugar is dissolved.
2 Bring to a rolling boil over a high heat, then remove from the heat.
3 Add the brandy and whisk to incorporate. Pour into an airtight container and leave to cool completely. Once cooled, the brandy syrup is ready for use and will keep in the refrigerator for 6 months.

Elderflower Syrup

Makes 700 g (1 lb 9 oz)
Time 2 days

10	fresh elderflower heads
1	lemon
350 g	(12.4 oz) caster (superfine) sugar
350 g	(12.4 oz) water
5 g	(1 teaspoon) citric acid

Elderflowers are the true markers of the seasons shifting for me, and bring the hope of warmer weather. The blooms begin appearing in the middle of May – just before Shane's birthday.

Day one

1 Once you've sourced and picked your elderflowers, steep the flower heads in cold water for 1 hour. This will kill any small insects living on the stalks, stems or flowers.
2 Drain the flower heads and give them a gentle shake to remove excess water. Pick the blooms from the stalks and place in a large bowl. Peel the lemon and add the rind to the bowl.
3 To make the syrup, combine the sugar and water in a saucepan and bring to a rapid boil for 1 minute.
4 Pour the syrup over the elderflowers and lemon. Cover the bowl with a large plate or the lid of a saucepan. Leave somewhere cool to infuse for 12–24 hours.

Day two

1 Strain the syrup into a saucepan with a fine sieve (strainer). Bring back to a rapid boil for 1 minute. Add the citric acid and taste. Depending on your palette and the elderflower season, you may need to add another pinch.
2 Store in an airtight container or sterilised bottle (see page 192) with a tight-fitting lid. Keep in the refrigerator and consume within 2 months.

Brown Butter

Makes 80 g (2.8 oz)
Time 20 minutes

100 g	(3.5 oz) unsalted butter

This brown butter is used for our *Everything Croissants* (see page 54).

1 Start melting the butter in a medium saucepan over a medium heat. The size of the saucepan is important as the butter will begin to foam, increasing in volume and voracity. As the butter melts, stir occasionally with a heatproof rubber spatula, scraping the bottom of the pan and agitating the milk solids. The water in the butter will begin to evaporate and the liquid gold will boil.

2 As the water evaporates, the milk solids will begin to brown and caramelise. This can happen very quickly, so keep a watchful eye on the pan. Once the butter has a nutty brown colour you are happy with, remove the pan from the heat. The butter will continue to colour in the retained heat of the fats.

3 Strain the butter into a metal bowl. Never use plastic, as brown butter can reach surprisingly high temperatures and melt or warp containers. Brown butter will solidify in the refrigerator and can be kept in airtight container for 2 weeks.

Egg Wash

Makes 245 g (8.6 oz)
Time 10 minutes

50 g	(1.8 oz) egg (1 UK medium egg/US large egg)
140 g	(4.9 oz) egg yolk (7 egg UK medium/US large eggs)
40–45 g	(1.4–1.6 oz) cream
5 g	(1 teaspoon) whole milk

An egg wash gives pastry a lovely sheen – try using this on our *Irish Butter Croissants* (see page 31) and *Pains au Chocolat* (see page 39).

Using a hand-held blender, emulsify all the ingredients together. The egg wash can be kept in an airtight container in the refrigerator for up to 5 days.

Carrot and Spring Onion Kimchi

Makes 900 g (2 lb)
Time 4–6 days

550 g	(19.4 oz/about 1 head) Chinese leaf (napa cabbage)
11 g	(0.4 oz) fine sea salt
150 g	(5.3 oz) carrots
30 g	(1 oz/1 bunch) spring onions (scallions)
30 g	(1 oz) coriander (cilantro) leaves
75 g	(2.7 oz) radishes
30 g	(1 oz) dillisk seaweed (optional)
80 g	(2.8 oz) gochujang paste

Why not try your hand at making your own kimchi for our *Kimchi and Coolea Cheese Bear Claws* on page 50? You can add kimchi to fried rice, serve it on the side of your morning eggs, or create a quick bibimbap (a Korean rice dish made with steamed rice, stir-fried vegetables and a crispy fried egg.)

1 Wash and dry the cabbage, then cut in half and remove the core. Thinly slice into long strips.
2 Massage the cabbage and salt together with your hands in a large bowl for 5 minutes. This will help release the water from the cabbage. Place another bowl on top of the cabbage and weigh it down. Leave to macerate for 2 hours.
3 While the cabbage is macerating, prepare the other vegetables. Peel and grate the carrots. Top and tail the spring onions and thinly slice. Pick the coriander leaves from the stalks and thinly shred. Top and tail the radishes and grate.
4 Soak the dillisk seaweed (if using) in cold water to rehydrate. Drain off the water and pat the seaweed dry. Chop into large pieces.
5 Drain the cabbage, reserving 100 g (3.5 oz) of the water for later. Rinse the cabbage and pat dry. Return to the large mixing bowl.
6 Toss the carrot, spring onion, coriander, radish and gochujang paste into the cabbage. Add more gochujang if you would like the kimchi extra spicy. Taste as you go. Use your hands to evenly coat all the vegetables with the paste. Mix in the chopped seaweed.
7 Pack the kimchi tightly into sterilised jars (see page 192), pressing down firmly to squeeze out any air bubbles. You want the vegetables to be submerged in the liquid. If there isn't enough liquid from the vegetables, top up the jar with the reserved cabbage water. Leave 2.5 cm (1 in) at the top of the jar for the release of air bubbles.
8 Put the lids on the jars tightly and leave at room temperature for 3–5 days. Each day, release the gas building up in the jars and taste the kimchi. The longer the kimchi sits at room temperature, the more sour it will be.
9 Once you are happy with the tang and flavour of the kimichi, transfer the jars to the refrigerator where it will continue to ferment and age but at a much slower, steady rate.

Tomatillo, Ginger and Chilli Relish

Makes 5–6 x 220 g (7.8 oz) jars
Time 2 hours

1.1 kg	(1 lb 7.5 oz) tomatillos
25 g	(0.9 oz) red chillies
265 g	(9.3 oz) lime juice
265 g	(9.3 oz) peeled and grated fresh ginger
385 g	(13.5 oz) caster (superfine) sugar

This relish recipe was created by my mum, Mary, when she received a glut of McNally Family Farm tomatillos one autumn and did not want them to go to waste. It's a tangy relish, with a fiery kick from fresh ginger. We jar this up in late summer and early autumn when Irish-grown tomatillos are at their peak. It's the perfect match for a toasted sandwich or dolloped on top of eggs and avocado on sourdough. And it's very cheeky with a fried egg, garlicky greens and sausages. It also makes a delicious accompaniment to a cheese board, from a creamy goat's cheese to a robust blue. Or try serving it with our *Pork, Apple and Mustard Sausage Rolls* (see page 182). This recipe makes six jars, so give them as gifts to family and friends if you don't think you will use them all.

1. Peel the husks from the tomatillos and wash them thoroughly. They will have a sticky residue on their flesh from the husks. Treat them as you would a tomato: cut in half and chop into 2.5 cm (1 in) pieces.
2. Remove the seeds from the chillies and finely chop. Depending on your spice tolerance, you can opt to leave the seeds in.
3. Put the chopped tomatillos, lime juice, ginger and chillies into a heavy-based saucepan or preserving pan. Cook over a medium-low heat for 10 minutes. The tomatillos will break down and the colour will shift from electric green to a paler sage colour.
4. Add the sugar and increase the heat. The mixture will begin to bubble rapidly, as the juices from the tomatillos evaporate. It can spit and hiss at you, so be careful of your hands and arms.
5. Stir continuously until the mixture has a thick, chutney-like consistency. Ideally, it should reach 103.5–105°C (218–221°F) on a digital thermometer.
6. Pour the relish into warm, sterilised jars (see page 192) and seal immediately with tight-fitting lids. Store in a cool, dark place. The relish will keep for 6–9 months. Once opened, store in the refrigerator.

Everything Seed Mix

Makes 1 small jar
Time 4 hours 30 minutes

4	garlic cloves, finely chopped
60 g	(2 oz) spring onions (scallions) (about 2 bunches), thinly sliced
20 g	(0.7 oz) poppy seeds
60 g	(2 oz) white sesame seeds
60 g	(2 oz) black sesame seeds
10 g	(0.4 oz) flaky sea salt

This seed mix is used for our wonderful *Everything Croissants* (see page 54).

1 Spread out the garlic and spring onions in a thin, even layer on a dehydrator tray. If you don't have a dehydrator, use your oven. Spread the garlic and spring onion in a thin layer on a baking sheet lined with baking parchment and set the oven as low as you can – 70°C (160°F) would be ideal.
2 Dehydrate the garlic and spring onion until completely dried. This should take approximately 4 hours. The garlic and spring onions will shrink dramatically in volume, but don't worry as they still pack a punch.
3 Once dry, blitz into a fine powder in a spice grinder or food processor. You could also use a pestle and mortar.
4 Combine the garlic and spring onion powder in a small bowl with the poppy seeds, white and black sesame seeds and salt. Transfer to a well-sealed jar or airtight container. The seed mix will keep for up to 3 months.

Labneh

Makes 650 g (1 lb 7 oz)
Time 2 days

1 kg	(2 lb 4 oz) full-fat Greek yoghurt
7.5 g	(1½ teaspoons) fine sea salt

Labneh has deep roots in Middle Eastern countries such as Lebanon, Syria, Palestine and Turkey. It is made by straining yoghurt to remove most of the whey, resulting in a thick, creamy and smooth fresh cheese. The addition of salt is important, as it helps to coagulate the proteins and release the liquid whey. The straining process intensifies the yoghurt's flavour, so use something that's high quality. This labneh forms the base of the cream cheese filling in our *Everything Croissants* (see page 54). We also use labneh for our *Basque Cheesecake* (see page 89) in place of shop-bought cream cheese.

Day one

1 Combine the yoghurt and salt in a large mixing bowl.
2 Set a fsieve (fine-mesh strainer) lined with a piece of muslin (cheesecloth) over a container or mixing bowl. Leave to strain for 24 hours in the refrigerator.

Day two

1 The ratio of whey to strained labneh will vary throughout the year, as the fat content of yoghurt shifts. From 1 kg (2 lb 4 oz) Greek yoghurt you should yield approximately 600 g (1 lb 5 oz) strained labneh and 390 g (13.8 oz) whey. Discard the whey. The labneh will keep in the refrigerator for 7 days.

Togarashi

Makes 1 small jar
Time 4 hours 30 minutes

---

28 g	(0.9 oz) dillisk seaweed
125 g	(4.4 oz) gochujang paste
20 g	(0.7 oz) coriander (cilantro)
50 g	(1.8 oz) kimchi juice (from a jar of shop-bought kimchi)
25 g	(0.9 oz) tamari
2 g	(½ teaspoon) freshly ground black pepper
30 g	(1 oz) white sesame seeds, toasted
30 g	(1 oz) black sesame seeds, toasted

Flaky sea salt

---

1. Place the seaweed in a small bowl of cold water for 10 minutes to rehydrate. Drain the water and pat the seaweed dry.
2. Place the seaweed, gochujang paste, coriander, kimchi juice, tamari and black pepper in a food processor. Pulse the ingredients together.
3. Spread the mixture in a thin layer on dehydrator trays. If you don't have a dehydrator, use your oven. Spread the mixture in a thin layer on a baking sheet lined with baking parchment and set the oven as low as you can – 70°C (160°F) would be ideal.
4. Dehydrate on low until completely crisp. This should take approximately 4 hours. Blitz the seaweed mix in a spice grinder or crush with a pestle and mortar.
5. Add the toasted sesame seeds to the seaweed mix. Check for seasoning, adding sea salt according to taste. This will vary with each recipe, depending on how salty the kimchi juice is.
6. Store the togarashi in an airtight container or sterilised jar (see page 192) with a tight-fitting lid. The togarashi will keep for 1 month.

EVERYTHING CROISSANT
APPLE CRUMBLE
MORNING BUN

CARDAMOM
HONEY BUN

Glossary

Autolyse
Autolyse is a bread-making technique in which flour and water are mixed and left to rest before adding salt, yeast or a sourdough levain. This process allows enzymes in the flour to break starches down into sugars and proteins into gluten, improving dough extensibility, hydration and flavour. Typically lasting 20 minutes to an hour, it facilitates easier kneading and enhances the bread's texture and crumb structure.

Bain-marie (double boiler)
A hot water bath used for delicate food preparation such as melted chocolate, curds, custards and sauces. A heatproof bowl is placed over a saucepan of simmering water and the ingredients are heated in the bowl.

Baker's percentage
A calculation whereby the weight of every ingredient is calculated as a percentage of the weight of the flour. It allows you to scale up or down batch sizes effortlessly.

Banneton (proving basket)
A proving basket used to hold dough as it rests and ferments. They can be made from rattan, wicker, plastic or even wood pulp. Available in a variety of shapes, sizes and capacity.

Bâtard loaf
A French term for an oblong or oval shaped loaf.

Beurrage
The butter block used for laminating pastries.

Blind baking
A method of pre-cooking pastry without any filling. It involves lining the pastry with baking parchment and weighing it down with baking beans (pie weights). The weights stop the pastry from expanding so that it keeps its shape.

Bloom (gelatine)
To hydrate gelatine (powdered or sheet) so that it is softened and melts evenly into custards, creams and fillings.

Bulk fermentation
The first stage of proving dough, in which it ferments as one single mass before being divided and shaped. Also referred to as the first rise, primary fermentation, bulk rise or bulk prove.

Crème diplomat
A mixture of crème pâtissière and unsweetened whipped cream.

Crème pâtissière (pastry cream)
A thick, creamy custard that has the addition of starch to help set it.

Crémeux
A light custard emulsified with chocolate (white, milk or dark) to create a rich, stable filling that can be piped, poured into moulds or whipped.

Emulsion/emulsify
To blend together ingredients that don't normally mix well.

Flaky pastry
A variation on puff pastry in which cold chunks of butter are mixed into pastry and a sequence of turns develop the layers. Also known as rough puff.

Float test
The float test is used to check the readiness of a sourdough levain or levain. A small amount of levain is gently dropped into a bowl of water. If it floats, this indicates the levain has developed sufficient gas and is ready to be used for baking. If it sinks, it may need more time to ferment or could be underfed.

Galette
A French, rustic-style, free-form tart, topped with either sweet or savoury fillings.

Ganache
A mixture of melted chocolate and cream. Once set it is smooth, rich and glossy.

Hand-laminate
To roll out delicate layers of pastry and butter by hand to create croissant or puff pastry dough.

Levain
Levain is a key building block in sourdough bread baking. It is preferment made of wild yeast, bacteria, flour and water. It gives sourdough its quintessential tang and strength to slowly rise. It is also referred to as sourdough starter, mother, culture or leaven.

Maceration
To soak raw or dried fruit (or vegetables) in a liquid, allowing them to soften while taking on the flavours from that liquid. When used for soft fruits such as strawberries, raspberries or rhubarb, they will release their own liquids to steep in.

Noyau (pl. noyaux)
Kernel of stone fruits like apricots, cherries, nectarines or peaches.

Osmotolerant yeast
A special strain of yeast that performs well in high-sugar doughs with a lower volume of water.

Rocher
Also known as a one-handed quenelle, this is a technique for shaping soft foods such as ice cream or cream into an oval shape using a spoon.

Temper
A method in custard preparation in which a portion of the hot cream/milk is poured onto the egg mixture before combining the two together. It prevents the eggs from getting a shock from the heat and curdling.

Viennoiserie
French breakfast pastries such as croissant, pain au chocolat, pain au raisin.

Yudane
A roux made from milk or water and flour that is precooked before being added to Japanese milk bread. It aids a soft, delicate, light crumb structure.

Acknowledgements

It really does take a village to run a bakery business. And in the same breath, it takes a village to write and publish a baking book.

Shane, what can I say; thank you for your love and support through everything. It is total madness to open a bakery, have a baby and write a book in the same year. Thank you for steadying the ship at the bakery, allowing me the time to recipe test and write at home. For making me laugh and always bringing me down a notch when starting to spiral with my endless to-do lists.

This book would not have become a reality if it wasn't for Kate at Quadrille. Thank you for coming to me and Shane with the idea of a Scéal baking book in 2021, for your guidance through several publishing pitches, for coaching me on how to write a book and for always cheering me on.

Kitty Coles, the Scéal book idea wouldn't have popped up for Kate if it wasn't for you hyping about Scéal at London photoshoots. Without you chatting about us around town, this book might not have ever materialised. Thank you for keeping the book shoot days calm and effortless.

My mum, Mary, for not batting an eyelid for the endless hours of childcare you did with Robin Mimi, so I could write this book in a baby-free house. I'm so grateful for the hours you spent walking Robin to sleep around Greystones, hail, rain or shine.

Our darling friend, Cissy. You came to Scéal for a week-long stage and stayed for four years. Thank you for your dedication to Scéal – you helped shape our bakery to what it is today. Thank you for not hesitating to set aside time to fly back to Ireland to shoot this book with us – we missed having you around. Thank you for testing the recipes and all the encouragement to keep going.

Shantanu, our dear friend, thank you for beautifully capturing Scéal since the very beginning. Your keen eye for detail has moulded the aesthetic of our bakery more than you'll ever know.

Even though we never met in person, thank you, Tegan, for instantly understanding the design and aesthetic of the Scéal book. Thank you for taking my rambling emails and making them into something so beautilful.

Caroline, thank you for reading my meandering manuscript, giving shape to my notes and for editing all my baby-brain spelling mistakes. The book flows beautifully thanks to your watchful eye.

To our team at Scéal: you are the most talented, dedicated, hard-working group of people I know. Thank you for taking our idea of Scéal bakery and running with it wholeheartedly. It is no easy feat to open the doors of the bakery seven days a week – there are so many moving parts in a business like ours – and this is down to all our your tireless work.

To our wonderful customers, past and present: I know we say this all the time, but we really wouldn't be where we are now if it wasn't for your support. You followed us around Dublin for years, according to our continuously moving market-stall schedule. To our community in Greystones: you welcomed us with open arms, warmth and curiousity. Thank you with all our hearts for embracing us and everything we do.

To our suppliers: I'm so grateful for you making time in your busy calenders to allow us to shoot with you. Kyle and Jack from OpenHive, James from Malone Fruit Farm and Robert from Kells Wholemeal. You provide constant inspiration for my menu ideas.

Fermoyle Pottery, Mangan Studios and Araucaria Ceramics, thank you for your skillful hands that made the ceramics used for photographing this book.

About the Authors

Charlotte Leonard-Kane and Shane Palmer, partners in life and in business, are the founders of Scéal, an Irish bakery in the coastal town of Greystones that specialises in using local and seasonal ingredients to superpower the flavours of their breads and pastries.

Index

D

E

F

G

R

S

T

V

W

Y

Quadrille, Penguin Random House UK, One Embassy Gardens, 8 Viaduct Gardens, London SW11 7BW

Quadrille Publishing Limited is part of the Penguin Random House group of companies whose addresses can be found at global.penguinrandomhouse.com

Penguin Random House UK

Published by Quadrille in 2025

www.penguin.co.uk

A CIP catalogue record for this book is available from the British Library

ISBN 9781837833658
10 9 8 7 6 5 4 3 2 1

Managing Director, Publishing
Sarah Lavelle

Publishing Director
Kajal Mistry

Senior Commissioning Editor
Kate Burkett

Copy Editor
Caroline West

Proofreader
Lucy Kingett

Indexer
Cathy Heath

Designer
Tegan Ella Hendel

Photographer
Shantanu Starick

Food Stylist
Kitty Coles

Food Stylist Assistant
Cissy Difford

Head of Production
Stephen Lang

Senior Production Controller
Martina Georgieva

Colour reproduction by p2d

Printed in China by C&C Offset Printing Co., Ltd.

The authorised representative in the EEA is Penguin Random House Ireland, Morrison Chambers, 32 Nassau Street, Dublin D02 YH68.

MIX
Paper | Supporting responsible forestry
FSC www.fsc.org FSC® C018179

Penguin Random House is committed to a sustainable future for our business, our readers and our planet. This book is made from Forest Stewardship Council® certified paper.